# Ice Cream Recipe Book

200+ Artisan Gelato Recipes to

Make at Home

Christina Torres

Copyright © 2023 - All rights reserved.

The content contained within this book may not be reproduced, duplicated, or transmitted without direct written permission from the author or the publisher.

Under no circumstances will any blame or legal responsibility be held against the publisher, or author, for any damages, reparation, or monetary loss due to the information contained within this book. Either directly or indirectly.

**Legal Notice:**

This book is copyright protected. This book is only for personal use. You cannot amend, distribute, sell, use, quote, or paraphrase any part, or the content within this book, without the consent of the author or publisher.

**Disclaimer Notice:**

Please note the information contained within this document is for educational and entertainment purposes only. All effort has been executed to present accurate, up-to-date, and reliable, complete information. No warranties of any kind are declared or implied. Readers acknowledge that the author is not engaging in the rendering of legal, financial, medical, or professional advice. The content within this book has been derived from various sources. Please consult a licensed professional before attempting any techniques outlined in this book.

By reading this document, the reader agrees that under no circumstances is the author responsible for any losses, direct or indirect, which are incurred as a result of the use of the information contained within this document, including, but not limited to, — errors, omissions, or inaccuracies.

# Table of the Contents:

**Fruit Ice Cream** .................................................................. 14

1. Strawberry Sorbet ........................................................... 14
2. Mango Gelato .................................................................. 14
3. Raspberry Gelato ............................................................ 15
4. Peach Sorbet ................................................................... 16
5. Blueberry Sorbet ............................................................. 16
6. Watermelon Sorbet ........................................................ 17
7. Pineapple Gelato ............................................................ 17
8. Cherry Gelato .................................................................. 18
9. Kiwi Sorbet ...................................................................... 19
10. Banana Gelato ............................................................... 19
11. Pomegranate Sorbet .................................................... 20
12. Coconut Gelato ............................................................. 20
13. Blackberry Sorbet ......................................................... 21
14. Apricot Gelato ............................................................... 22
15. Lime Sorbet .................................................................... 22
16. Pear Sorbet .................................................................... 23
17. Passion Fruit Gelato ..................................................... 23
18. Raspberry-Lemon Gelato ............................................ 24
19. Plum Sorbet ................................................................... 25
20. Grapefruit Sorbet .......................................................... 25

21. Lemon Sorbet ............................................................. 26
22. Mixed Berry Gelato ................................................. 26
23. Guava Sorbet ............................................................ 27
24. Lychee Gelato ........................................................... 28
25. Orange Sorbet .......................................................... 28
26. Papaya Sorbet .......................................................... 29
27. Mango-Lime Gelato ................................................ 29
28. Fig Sorbet .................................................................. 30
29. Blueberry Gelato ..................................................... 31
30. Avocado Gelato ....................................................... 31
31. Grape Sorbet ............................................................ 32
32. Tangerine Gelato ..................................................... 33
33. Pineapple-Mint Gelato ........................................... 33
34. Coconut-Pineapple Gelato .................................... 34
35. Blackcurrant Sorbet ................................................ 35
36. Raspberry Sorbet .................................................... 35
37. Apricot Gelato II ...................................................... 36
38. Pomegranate Sorbet II .......................................... 37
39. Blackberry Gelato ................................................... 37
40. Cherry Sorbet ........................................................... 38
41. Plum Sorbet II .......................................................... 38
42. Peach Gelato ............................................................ 39
43. Dragon Fruit Sorbet ............................................... 40

44. Strawberry-Banana Gelato ............................................................. 40

45. Cucumber-Lime Sorbet ................................................................. 41

46. Passion Fruit Gelato II .................................................................. 42

47. White Peach Sorbet ..................................................................... 42

48. Fig and Honey Gelato .................................................................. 43

49. Tangerine Sorbet ......................................................................... 44

50. Cantaloupe Gelato ...................................................................... 44

51. Papaya Sorbet .............................................................................. 45

52. Fig Gelato ..................................................................................... 46

53. Honeydew Sorbet ........................................................................ 46

54. Apple Gelato ................................................................................ 47

55. Cherry and Vanilla Gelato ........................................................... 48

56. Pomegranate Gelato ................................................................... 48

57. Guava Gelato ............................................................................... 49

58. Kiwi Gelato ................................................................................... 50

59. Mango Sorbet .............................................................................. 50

60. Cantaloupe Melon Sorbet .......................................................... 51

**Chocolate Ice Cream** ........................................................................ 52

61. Classic Chocolate Gelato ............................................................ 52

62. Chocolate Mint Gelato ................................................................ 53

63. Chocolate Orange Gelato ........................................................... 53

64. Mocha Gelato .............................................................................. 54

65. Chocolate Chili Gelato ................................................................ 54

66. Chocolate Raspberry Swirl Gelato ........................................... 55
67. Chocolate Coconut Gelato ...................................................... 55
68. Chocolate Hazelnut Gelato ..................................................... 56
69. Chocolate Peanut Butter Gelato ............................................. 56
70. Chocolate Banana Gelato........................................................ 57
71. Chocolate Avocado Gelato...................................................... 57
72. Salted Caramel Chocolate Gelato .......................................... 58
73. Chocolate Almond Gelato ...................................................... 59
74. Chocolate Amaretto Gelato ................................................... 59
75. Chocolate Cherry Gelato ........................................................ 60
76. Chocolate Pistachio Gelato .................................................... 60
77. Chocolate Marshmallow Gelato ............................................ 61
78. Chocolate Tiramisu Gelato .................................................... 61
79. Chocolate Blueberry Gelato ................................................... 62
80. Chocolate Cookie Gelato ....................................................... 63
81. Chocolate Pecan Gelato ......................................................... 63
82. Chocolate Caramel Swirl Gelato ............................................ 64
83. Chocolate and Toasted Almond Gelato ................................. 64
84. Chocolate Macadamia Gelato ............................................... 65
85. Chocolate and Candied Orange Peel Gelato ......................... 66
86. Dark Chocolate and Mint Gelato............................................ 66
87. Chocolate and Roasted Cashew Gelato................................. 67
88. Chocolate and Ginger Gelato ................................................ 67

89. Chocolate and Raisin Gelato ................................................................. 68

90. Chocolate and Mocha Gelato ................................................................ 69

91. Chocolate and Coconut Gelato ............................................................. 69

92. Chocolate Banana Gelato II .................................................................. 70

93. Chocolate and Caramelized Hazelnut Gelato .................................... 70

94. Chocolate and Honeycomb Gelato ...................................................... 71

95. Chocolate and Chili Gelato .................................................................... 72

96. Chocolate and Raspberry Gelato ......................................................... 72

97. Chocolate and Candied Ginger Gelato ............................................... 73

98. Chocolate and Walnut Gelato ............................................................... 73

99. Chocolate and Bourbon Gelato ............................................................ 74

100. Chocolate and Salted Caramel Gelato .............................................. 75

**Coffee Ice Cream** ........................................................................................ 76

101. Classic Coffee Gelato ........................................................................... 76

102. Coffee and Cinnamon Gelato ............................................................. 77

103. Coffee and Vanilla Gelato ................................................................... 77

104. Coffee and Hazelnut Gelato ............................................................... 78

105. Coffee and Caramel Gelato ................................................................ 78

106. Coffee and Chocolate Chip Gelato .................................................... 79

107. Coffee and Almond Gelato .................................................................. 79

108. Coffee and Coconut Gelato ................................................................. 80

109. Coffee and Irish Cream Gelato ........................................................... 81

110. Coffee and Whiskey Gelato ................................................................. 81

111. Coffee and Toffee Gelato ......................................................... 82

112. Coffee and Banana Gelato ..................................................... 82

113. Coffee and Cardamom Gelato ............................................... 83

114. Coffee and Pistachio Gelato ................................................... 84

115. Coffee and Cherry Gelato ....................................................... 84

116. Coffee and Rum Gelato .......................................................... 85

117. Coffee and Peppermint Gelato ............................................... 85

118. Coffee and Peanut Butter Gelato ........................................... 86

119. Coffee and Maple Syrup Gelato ............................................. 87

120. Coffee and Oreo Gelato .......................................................... 87

121. Classic Coffee Ice Cream ........................................................ 88

122. Vegan Coffee Coconut Milk Ice Cream ................................. 89

123. Mocha Chip Ice Cream ........................................................... 89

124. Coffee and Coconut Milk Gelato ........................................... 90

125. Coffee and Marshmallow Gelato ........................................... 91

126. Iced Coffee Sorbet ................................................................... 92

127. Coffee and Dark Chocolate Chip Gelato ............................... 92

128. Coffee and Macadamia Nut Gelato ....................................... 93

129. Coffee and Amaretto Gelato .................................................. 94

130. Coffee and Honey Gelato ....................................................... 94

131. Coffee and Bourbon Gelato .................................................... 95

132. Coffee and Mint Chocolate Chip Gelato ............................... 95

133. Coffee and Pecan Gelato ........................................................ 96

134. Coffee and White Chocolate Chip Gelato ............ 97
135. Espresso and Pistachio Swirl Gelato ............ 97
136. Cappuccino and Spiced Rum Gelato ............ 98
137. Mocha and Almond Butter Gelato ............ 99
138. Coffee and Coconut Flakes Gelato ............ 100
139. Coffee and Vanilla Bean Gelato ............ 101
140. Coffee and Hazelnut Liqueur Gelato ............ 101
141. Coffee and Dulce de Leche Gelato ............ 102
142. Turkish Coffee Ice Cream ............ 103
143. Coffee and Bailey's Gelato ............ 103
144. Coffee and Toasted Marshmallow Gelato ............ 104
145. Coffee and Toffee Bits Gelato ............ 105
146. Coffee and Salted Caramel Gelato ............ 105
147. Vietnamese Coffee Ice Cream ............ 106
148. Coffee Toffee Ice Cream ............ 107
149. Coffee and Caramelised Hazelnuts Gelato ............ 107
150. Espresso Gelato ............ 108

**Vegetable Ice Cream** ............ 110

151. Spinach and Kiwi Gelato ............ 110
152. Avocado Gelato ............ 110
153. Sweet Corn and Honey Gelato ............ 111
154. Sweet Potato and Cinnamon Gelato ............ 112
155. Zucchini and Mint Gelato ............ 113

156. Beetroot and Orange Gelato ..................................................113

157. Pumpkin and Spice Gelato ....................................................114

158. Carrot and Ginger Gelato .....................................................115

159. Red Bell Pepper and Basil Gelato .........................................115

160. Cucumber and Lime Gelato .................................................116

161. Tomato and Basil Gelato .....................................................117

162. Celery and Apple Gelato .....................................................117

163. Kale and Banana Gelato ......................................................118

164. Pea and Mint Gelato ...........................................................118

165. Fennel and Pear Gelato .......................................................119

166. Zucchini and Lemon Gelato ................................................120

167. Spinach and Pineapple Gelato ............................................120

168. Butternut Squash and Nutmeg Gelato ................................121

169. Sweet Corn Ice Cream ........................................................122

170. Broccoli and Kiwi Gelato .....................................................122

171. Avocado and Lime Gelato ...................................................123

172. Cucumber and Mint Gelato .................................................124

173. Pumpkin and Ginger Gelato ................................................124

174. Spinach and Mint Ice Cream ...............................................125

175. Beetroot Raspberry Sorbet .................................................126

**Toppings for Ice Cream** ...........................................................128

176. Chocolate Fudge Sauce ......................................................128

177. Salted Caramel Sauce .........................................................128

178. Berry Compote ............................................................... 129

179. Toasted Coconut Flakes ................................................. 130

180. Praline Pecans ............................................................... 130

181. Peanut Butter Drizzle .................................................... 131

182. Rainbow Sprinkles ........................................................ 131

183. Cherry Sauce ................................................................ 132

184. Candied Almonds ......................................................... 132

185. Whipped Cream ........................................................... 133

186. Marshmallow Fluff ....................................................... 133

187. Mocha Drizzle ............................................................... 134

188. Oreo Cookie Crumble ................................................... 134

189. White Chocolate Chips ................................................. 135

190. Cinnamon-Sugar Pecans .............................................. 135

191. Brownie Bites ............................................................... 136

192. Mint Syrup ................................................................... 136

193. Crushed Peppermint Candy ......................................... 137

194. Banana Slices ............................................................... 137

195. Crumbled Graham Crackers ......................................... 138

196. Matcha Sauce ............................................................... 138

197. Pistachio Crunch .......................................................... 139

198. Coconut Flakes ............................................................. 139

199. Spiced Honey Nut Topping .......................................... 140

200. Fresh Berries ................................................................ 141

201. Caramelized Bananas ....................................................................... 141
202. Cookie Dough Bites .......................................................................... 142
203. Blueberry Sauce ............................................................................... 142
204. Coconut Whipped Cream ................................................................ 143
205. Pomegranate Seeds ......................................................................... 143

# Fruit Ice Cream

## 1. Strawberry Sorbet

**Ingredients:**

- 500 grams of fresh strawberries
- 150 grams of granulated sugar
- Juice of 1 lemon

**Directions:**

1. Clean the strawberries and remove the stems. Cut into small pieces.
2. In a blender, combine strawberries, sugar, and lemon juice. Blend until smooth.
3. Pour the mixture into an ice cream maker and churn according to the manufacturer's instructions.
4. Once the sorbet reaches the desired consistency, transfer it to a lidded container and freeze for at least 2 hours before serving.

**Calories:** Approx 100 kcal per serving (based on 6 servings)

## 2. Mango Gelato

**Ingredients:**

- 2 ripe mangoes
- 200 ml of coconut milk
- 100 grams of sugar

**Directions:**

1. Peel the mangoes, remove the pits and cut into small pieces.
2. Put the mango pieces, coconut milk, and sugar into a blender. Blend until smooth.
3. Pour the mixture into an ice cream maker and churn according to the manufacturer's instructions.
4. Once the gelato is thick and creamy, transfer it to a lidded container and freeze for at least 2 hours before serving.

**Calories:** Approx 140 kcal per serving (based on 6 servings)

# 3. Raspberry Gelato

**Ingredients:**

- 500 grams of fresh raspberries
- 200 grams of sugar
- Juice of 1/2 a lemon

**Directions:**

1. Wash the raspberries and pat them dry.
2. In a blender, blend the raspberries, sugar, and lemon juice until smooth.
3. Strain the mixture to remove seeds if desired.
4. Pour the mixture into an ice cream maker and churn as per the manufacturer's instructions.
5. Once the gelato is thick and creamy, transfer it to a lidded container and freeze for at least 2 hours before serving.

**Calories:** Approx 110 kcal per serving (based on 6 servings)

## 4. Peach Sorbet

**Ingredients:**

- 4 ripe peaches
- 150 grams of granulated sugar
- Juice of 1 lemon

**Directions:**

1. Peel the peaches, remove the pits, and cut them into small pieces.
2. Blend the peach pieces, sugar, and lemon juice in a blender until smooth.
3. Pour the mixture into an ice cream maker and churn according to the manufacturer's instructions.
4. Once the sorbet is of the desired consistency, transfer it to a lidded container and freeze for at least 2 hours before serving.

**Calories:** Approx 90 kcal per serving (based on 6 servings)

## 5. Blueberry Sorbet

**Ingredients:**

- 500 grams of fresh blueberries
- 150 grams of granulated sugar
- Juice of 1 lemon

**Directions:**

1. Rinse the blueberries and pat dry.
2. Blend the blueberries, sugar, and lemon juice in a blender until smooth.

3. Strain the mixture to remove skins if desired.
4. Pour the mixture into an ice cream maker and churn as per the manufacturer's instructions.
5. Once the sorbet is of the desired consistency, transfer it to a lidded container and freeze for at least 2 hours before serving.

**Calories:** Approx 100 kcal per serving (based on 6 servings)

# 6. Watermelon Sorbet

**Ingredients:**

- 800 grams of seedless watermelon
- 150 grams of granulated sugar
- Juice of 1 lemon

**Directions:**

1. Cut the watermelon into small chunks, ensuring all seeds are removed.
2. In a blender, combine the watermelon chunks, sugar, and lemon juice. Blend until smooth.
3. Pour the mixture into an ice cream maker and churn according to the manufacturer's instructions.
4. Once the sorbet reaches the desired consistency, transfer it to a lidded container and freeze for at least 2 hours before serving.

**Calories:** Approx 80 kcal per serving (based on 6 servings)

# 7. Pineapple Gelato

**Ingredients:**

- 1 medium pineapple

- 150 grams of sugar
- 200 ml of coconut milk

**Directions:**

1. Peel the pineapple and cut into small chunks.
2. In a blender, combine the pineapple, sugar, and coconut milk. Blend until smooth.
3. Pour the mixture into an ice cream maker and churn according to the manufacturer's instructions.
4. Once the gelato is thick and creamy, transfer it to a lidded container and freeze for at least 2 hours before serving.

**Calories:** Approx 150 kcal per serving (based on 6 servings)

# 8. Cherry Gelato

**Ingredients:**

- 500 grams of cherries
- 200 grams of sugar
- 200 ml of almond milk

**Directions:**

1. Pit the cherries and cut into halves.
2. In a blender, combine the cherries, sugar, and almond milk. Blend until smooth.
3. Pour the mixture into an ice cream maker and churn according to the manufacturer's instructions.
4. Once the gelato is thick and creamy, transfer it to a lidded container and freeze for at least 2 hours before serving.

**Calories:** Approx 130 kcal per serving (based on 6 servings)

## 9. Kiwi Sorbet

**Ingredients:**

- 8 ripe kiwis
- 150 grams of granulated sugar
- Juice of 1 lemon

**Directions:**

1. Peel the kiwis and cut them into small pieces.
2. In a blender, blend the kiwi pieces, sugar, and lemon juice until smooth.
3. Pour the mixture into an ice cream maker and churn according to the manufacturer's instructions.
4. Once the sorbet is of the desired consistency, transfer it to a lidded container and freeze for at least 2 hours before serving.

**Calories:** Approx 100 kcal per serving (based on 6 servings)

## 10. Banana Gelato

**Ingredients:**

- 4 ripe bananas
- 100 grams of sugar
- 200 ml of almond milk

**Directions:**

1. Peel the bananas and cut them into small pieces.
2. Blend the banana pieces, sugar, and almond milk in a blender until smooth.

3. Pour the mixture into an ice cream maker and churn as per the manufacturer's instructions.
4. Once the gelato is thick and creamy, transfer it to a lidded container and freeze for at least 2 hours before serving.

**Calories:** Approx 140 kcal per serving (based on 6 servings)

# 11. Pomegranate Sorbet

**Ingredients:**

- Juice of 4 large pomegranates
- 150 grams of granulated sugar
- Juice of 1 lemon

**Directions:**

1. Cut the pomegranates in half and juice them. You should have about 2 cups of pomegranate juice.
2. In a blender, combine the pomegranate juice, sugar, and lemon juice. Blend until the sugar is completely dissolved.
3. Pour the mixture into an ice cream maker and churn according to the manufacturer's instructions.
4. Once the sorbet reaches the desired consistency, transfer it to a lidded container and freeze for at least 2 hours before serving.

**Calories:** Approx 100 kcal per serving (based on 6 servings)

# 12. Coconut Gelato

**Ingredients:**

- 400 ml of coconut milk
- 150 grams of sugar

- 100 ml of coconut cream

**Directions:**

1. In a blender, combine the coconut milk, sugar, and coconut cream. Blend until smooth.
2. Pour the mixture into an ice cream maker and churn according to the manufacturer's instructions.
3. Once the gelato is thick and creamy, transfer it to a lidded container and freeze for at least 2 hours before serving.

**Calories:** Approx 200 kcal per serving (based on 6 servings)

# 13. Blackberry Sorbet

**Ingredients:**

- 500 grams of fresh blackberries
- 150 grams of granulated sugar
- Juice of 1 lemon

**Directions:**

1. Rinse the blackberries and pat them dry.
2. In a blender, blend the blackberries, sugar, and lemon juice until smooth.
3. Strain the mixture to remove seeds if desired.
4. Pour the mixture into an ice cream maker and churn as per the manufacturer's instructions.
5. Once the sorbet is of the desired consistency, transfer it to a lidded container and freeze for at least 2 hours before serving.

**Calories:** Approx 90 kcal per serving (based on 6 servings)

## 14. Apricot Gelato

**Ingredients:**

- 6 ripe apricots
- 150 grams of sugar
- 200 ml of almond milk

**Directions:**

1. Cut the apricots in half, remove the pits, and cut them into small pieces.
2. Blend the apricot pieces, sugar, and almond milk in a blender until smooth.
3. Pour the mixture into an ice cream maker and churn as per the manufacturer's instructions.
4. Once the gelato is thick and creamy, transfer it to a lidded container and freeze for at least 2 hours before serving.

**Calories:** Approx 120 kcal per serving (based on 6 servings)

## 15. Lime Sorbet

**Ingredients:**

- Juice of 6 limes
- 150 grams of granulated sugar
- Zest of 2 limes

**Directions:**

1. In a blender, combine the lime juice, sugar, and lime zest. Blend until the sugar is completely dissolved.

2. Pour the mixture into an ice cream maker and churn according to the manufacturer's instructions.
3. Once the sorbet reaches the desired consistency, transfer it to a lidded container and freeze for at least 2 hours before serving.

**Calories:** Approx 80 kcal per serving (based on 6 servings)

# 16. Pear Sorbet

**Ingredients:**

- 4 ripe pears
- 150 grams of granulated sugar
- Juice of 1 lemon

**Directions:**

1. Peel the pears, remove the cores, and cut them into small pieces.
2. Blend the pear pieces, sugar, and lemon juice in a blender until smooth.
3. Pour the mixture into an ice cream maker and churn according to the manufacturer's instructions.
4. Once the sorbet is of the desired consistency, transfer it to a lidded container and freeze for at least 2 hours before serving.

**Calories:** Approx 90 kcal per serving (based on 6 servings)

# 17. Passion Fruit Gelato

**Ingredients:**

- Pulp of 10 passion fruits
- 150 grams of sugar
- 200 ml of coconut milk

**Directions:**

1. Scoop the pulp out of the passion fruits.
2. Blend the passion fruit pulp, sugar, and coconut milk in a blender until smooth.
3. Pour the mixture into an ice cream maker and churn as per the manufacturer's instructions.
4. Once the gelato is thick and creamy, transfer it to a lidded container and freeze for at least 2 hours before serving.

**Calories:** Approx 130 kcal per serving (based on 6 servings)

# 18. Raspberry-Lemon Gelato

**Ingredients:**

- 300 grams of fresh raspberries
- 150 grams of sugar
- Juice and zest of 2 lemons
- 200 ml of almond milk

**Directions:**

1. Rinse the raspberries and pat dry.
2. Blend the raspberries, sugar, lemon juice, lemon zest, and almond milk in a blender until smooth.
3. Pour the mixture into an ice cream maker and churn as per the manufacturer's instructions.
4. Once the gelato is thick and creamy, transfer it to a lidded container and freeze for at least 2 hours before serving.

**Calories:** Approx 110 kcal per serving (based on 6 servings)

# 19. Plum Sorbet

**Ingredients:**

- 6 ripe plums
- 150 grams of granulated sugar
- Juice of 1 lemon

**Directions:**

1. Cut the plums in half, remove the pits, and cut them into small pieces.
2. Blend the plum pieces, sugar, and lemon juice in a blender until smooth.
3. Pour the mixture into an ice cream maker and churn according to the manufacturer's instructions.
4. Once the sorbet is of the desired consistency, transfer it to a lidded container and freeze for at least 2 hours before serving.

**Calories:** Approx 80 kcal per serving (based on 6 servings)

# 20. Grapefruit Sorbet

**Ingredients:**

- Juice of 4 grapefruits
- 150 grams of granulated sugar
- Zest of 2 grapefruits

**Directions:**

1. In a blender, combine the grapefruit juice, sugar, and grapefruit zest. Blend until the sugar is completely dissolved.

2. Pour the mixture into an ice cream maker and churn according to the manufacturer's instructions.
3. Once the sorbet reaches the desired consistency, transfer it to a lidded container and freeze for at least 2 hours before serving.

**Calories:** Approx 90 kcal per serving (based on 6 servings)

# 21. Lemon Sorbet

**Ingredients:**

- Juice of 4 lemons
- 150 grams of granulated sugar
- Zest of 2 lemons

**Directions:**

1. In a blender, combine the lemon juice, sugar, and lemon zest. Blend until the sugar is completely dissolved.
2. Pour the mixture into an ice cream maker and churn according to the manufacturer's instructions.
3. Once the sorbet reaches the desired consistency, transfer it to a lidded container and freeze for at least 2 hours before serving.

**Calories:** Approx 80 kcal per serving (based on 6 servings)

# 22. Mixed Berry Gelato

**Ingredients:**

- 500 grams of mixed berries (raspberries, blueberries, strawberries)
- 200 grams of sugar
- 200 ml of almond milk

**Directions:**

1. Rinse the berries and pat them dry.
2. In a blender, blend the berries, sugar, and almond milk until smooth.
3. Strain the mixture to remove seeds if desired.
4. Pour the mixture into an ice cream maker and churn as per the manufacturer's instructions.
5. Once the gelato is thick and creamy, transfer it to a lidded container and freeze for at least 2 hours before serving.

**Calories:** Approx 120 kcal per serving (based on 6 servings)

# 23. Guava Sorbet

**Ingredients:**

- 500 grams of fresh guava
- 150 grams of granulated sugar
- Juice of 1 lemon

**Directions:**

1. Peel the guavas, remove the seeds, and cut them into small pieces.
2. Blend the guava pieces, sugar, and lemon juice in a blender until smooth.
3. Pour the mixture into an ice cream maker and churn according to the manufacturer's instructions.
4. Once the sorbet is of the desired consistency, transfer it to a lidded container and freeze for at least 2 hours before serving.

**Calories:** Approx 80 kcal per serving (based on 6 servings)

# 24. Lychee Gelato

**Ingredients:**

- 500 grams of fresh lychees
- 200 grams of sugar
- 200 ml of coconut milk

**Directions:**

1. Peel the lychees, remove the pits, and cut them into small pieces.
2. Blend the lychee pieces, sugar, and coconut milk in a blender until smooth.
3. Pour the mixture into an ice cream maker and churn as per the manufacturer's instructions.
4. Once the gelato is thick and creamy, transfer it to a lidded container and freeze for at least 2 hours before serving.

**Calories:** Approx 150 kcal per serving (based on 6 servings)

# 25. Orange Sorbet

**Ingredients:**

- Juice of 4 oranges
- 150 grams of granulated sugar
- Zest of 2 oranges

**Directions:**

1. In a blender, combine the orange juice, sugar, and orange zest. Blend until the sugar is completely dissolved.

2. Pour the mixture into an ice cream maker and churn according to the manufacturer's instructions.
3. Once the sorbet reaches the desired consistency, transfer it to a lidded container and freeze for at least 2 hours before serving.

**Calories:** Approx 80 kcal per serving (based on 6 servings)

## 26. Papaya Sorbet

**Ingredients:**

- 1 large ripe papaya
- 150 grams of granulated sugar
- Juice of 1 lemon

**Directions:**

1. Peel the papaya, remove the seeds, and cut it into small pieces.
2. Blend the papaya pieces, sugar, and lemon juice in a blender until smooth.
3. Pour the mixture into an ice cream maker and churn according to the manufacturer's instructions.
4. Once the sorbet is of the desired consistency, transfer it to a lidded container and freeze for at least 2 hours before serving.

**Calories:** Approx 80 kcal per serving (based on 6 servings)

## 27. Mango-Lime Gelato

**Ingredients:**

- 2 ripe mangoes
- 150 grams of sugar
- Juice and zest of 1 lime

- 200 ml of coconut milk

**Directions:**

1. Peel the mangoes, remove the pits, and cut them into small pieces.
2. Blend the mango pieces, sugar, lime juice, lime zest, and coconut milk in a blender until smooth.
3. Pour the mixture into an ice cream maker and churn as per the manufacturer's instructions.
4. Once the gelato is thick and creamy, transfer it to a lidded container and freeze for at least 2 hours before serving.

**Calories:** Approx 130 kcal per serving (based on 6 servings)

# 28. Fig Sorbet

**Ingredients:**

- 500 grams of fresh figs
- 150 grams of granulated sugar
- Juice of 1 lemon

**Directions:**

1. Cut the figs in half and remove the stems.
2. Blend the fig halves, sugar, and lemon juice in a blender until smooth.
3. Pour the mixture into an ice cream maker and churn according to the manufacturer's instructions.
4. Once the sorbet is of the desired consistency, transfer it to a lidded container and freeze for at least 2 hours before serving.

**Calories:** Approx 100 kcal per serving (based on 6 servings)

## 29. Blueberry Gelato

**Ingredients:**

- 500 grams of fresh blueberries
- 200 grams of sugar
- 200 ml of almond milk

**Directions:**

1. Rinse the blueberries and pat them dry.
2. Blend the blueberries, sugar, and almond milk in a blender until smooth.
3. Pour the mixture into an ice cream maker and churn as per the manufacturer's instructions.
4. Once the gelato is thick and creamy, transfer it to a lidded container and freeze for at least 2 hours before serving.

**Calories:** Approx 140 kcal per serving (based on 6 servings)

## 30. Avocado Gelato

**Ingredients:**

- 2 ripe avocados
- 150 grams of sugar
- 200 ml of coconut milk

**Directions:**

1. Cut the avocados in half, remove the pits, and scoop out the flesh.
2. Blend the avocado flesh, sugar, and coconut milk in a blender until smooth.

3. Pour the mixture into an ice cream maker and churn as per the manufacturer's instructions.
4. Once the gelato is thick and creamy, transfer it to a lidded container and freeze for at least 2 hours before serving.

**Calories:** Approx 220 kcal per serving (based on 6 servings)

# 31. Grape Sorbet

Ingredients:

- 500g of seedless grapes
- 150g sugar
- 100ml water
- Juice of 1 lemon

Directions:

1. Blend the grapes until smooth and strain the juice to remove any seeds or skin.
2. In a saucepan, heat the water and sugar until the sugar has dissolved, then let it cool.
3. Mix the grape juice, sugar syrup, and lemon juice together.
4. Pour the mixture into an ice cream maker and churn according to the manufacturer's instructions.
5. Transfer the sorbet to a lidded container and freeze for at least 2 hours before serving.

**Calories:** Approx 90 kcal per serving (based on 6 servings)

## 32. Tangerine Gelato

Ingredients:

- 1 cup tangerine juice
- 2/3 cup sugar
- 1 cup heavy cream
- 1 cup whole milk

Directions:

1. Combine the tangerine juice and sugar in a saucepan over medium heat, stirring until the sugar has dissolved.
2. Remove from heat and let it cool down.
3. Stir in the heavy cream and whole milk.
4. Pour the mixture into an ice cream maker and churn according to the manufacturer's instructions.
5. Transfer the gelato to a lidded container and freeze for at least 4 hours before serving.

**Calories:** Approx 102 kcal per serving (based on 6 servings)

## 33. Pineapple-Mint Gelato

Ingredients:

- 1 ripe pineapple
- 1 cup of sugar
- 1 cup heavy cream
- A handful of fresh mint leaves

Directions:

1. Peel and chop the pineapple, then blend it with the sugar and mint leaves until smooth.
2. Stir in the heavy cream.
3. Pour the mixture into an ice cream maker and churn according to the manufacturer's instructions.
4. Transfer the gelato to a lidded container and freeze for at least 4 hours before serving.

**Calories:** Approx 114 kcal per serving (based on 6 servings)

# 34. Coconut-Pineapple Gelato

**Ingredients:**

- 1 medium pineapple
- 150 grams of sugar
- 200 ml of coconut milk

**Directions:**

1. Peel the pineapple, remove the core, and cut it into small pieces.
2. Blend the pineapple pieces, sugar, and coconut milk in a blender until smooth.
3. Pour the mixture into an ice cream maker and churn as per the manufacturer's instructions.
4. Once the gelato is thick and creamy, transfer it to a lidded container and freeze for at least 2 hours before serving.

**Calories:** Approx 180 kcal per serving (based on 6 servings)

# 35. Blackcurrant Sorbet

Ingredients:

- 500g of blackcurrants
- 200g sugar
- 150ml water
- Juice of 1 lemon

Directions:

1. Blend the blackcurrants until smooth and strain the juice to remove any seeds.
2. In a saucepan, heat the water and sugar until the sugar has dissolved, then let it cool.
3. Mix the blackcurrant juice, sugar syrup, and lemon juice together.
4. Pour the mixture into an ice cream maker and churn according to the manufacturer's instructions.
5. Transfer the sorbet to a lidded container and freeze for at least 2 hours before serving.

**Calories:** Approx 90 kcal per serving (based on 6 servings)

# 36. Raspberry Sorbet

**Ingredients:**

- 500 grams of fresh raspberries
- 150 grams of granulated sugar
- Juice of 1 lemon

**Directions:**

1. Rinse the raspberries and pat them dry.
2. Blend the raspberries, sugar, and lemon juice in a blender until smooth.
3. Pour the mixture into an ice cream maker and churn according to the manufacturer's instructions.
4. Once the sorbet is of the desired consistency, transfer it to a lidded container and freeze for at least 2 hours before serving.

**Calories:** Approx 80 kcal per serving (based on 6 servings)

# 37. Apricot Gelato II

**Ingredients:**

- 500 grams of fresh apricots
- 200 grams of sugar
- 200 ml of almond milk

**Directions:**

1. Cut the apricots in half, remove the pits, and cut them into small pieces.
2. Blend the apricot pieces, sugar, and almond milk in a blender until smooth.
3. Pour the mixture into an ice cream maker and churn as per the manufacturer's instructions.
4. Once the gelato is thick and creamy, transfer it to a lidded container and freeze for at least 2 hours before serving.

**Calories:** Approx 130 kcal per serving (based on 6 servings)

# 38. Pomegranate Sorbet II

**Ingredients:**

- Juice of 4 pomegranates
- 150 grams of granulated sugar

**Directions:**

1. In a blender, combine the pomegranate juice and sugar. Blend until the sugar is completely dissolved.
2. Pour the mixture into an ice cream maker and churn according to the manufacturer's instructions.
3. Once the sorbet reaches the desired consistency, transfer it to a lidded container and freeze for at least 2 hours before serving.

**Calories:** Approx 90 kcal per serving (based on 6 servings)

# 39. Blackberry Gelato

**Ingredients:**

- 500 grams of fresh blackberries
- 200 grams of sugar
- 200 ml of almond milk

**Directions:**

1. Rinse the blackberries and pat them dry.
2. Blend the blackberries, sugar, and almond milk in a blender until smooth.

3. Pour the mixture into an ice cream maker and churn as per the manufacturer's instructions.
4. Once the gelato is thick and creamy, transfer it to a lidded container and freeze for at least 2 hours before serving.

**Calories:** Approx 140 kcal per serving (based on 6 servings)

# 40. Cherry Sorbet

**Ingredients:**

- 500 grams of fresh cherries
- 150 grams of granulated sugar
- Juice of 1 lemon

**Directions:**

1. Remove the pits from the cherries.
2. Blend the cherries, sugar, and lemon juice in a blender until smooth.
3. Pour the mixture into an ice cream maker and churn according to the manufacturer's instructions.
4. Once the sorbet is of the desired consistency, transfer it to a lidded container and freeze for at least 2 hours before serving.

**Calories:** Approx 90 kcal per serving (based on 6 servings)

# 41. Plum Sorbet II

**Ingredients:**

- 500 grams of fresh plums
- 150 grams of granulated sugar
- Juice of 1 lemon

**Directions:**

1. Cut the plums in half, remove the pits, and cut them into small pieces.
2. Blend the plum pieces, sugar, and lemon juice in a blender until smooth.
3. Pour the mixture into an ice cream maker and churn according to the manufacturer's instructions.
4. Once the sorbet is of the desired consistency, transfer it to a lidded container and freeze for at least 2 hours before serving.

**Calories:** Approx 90 kcal per serving (based on 6 servings)

## 42. Peach Gelato

**Ingredients:**

- 500 grams of fresh peaches
- 200 grams of sugar
- 200 ml of almond milk

**Directions:**

1. Cut the peaches in half, remove the pits, and cut them into small pieces.
2. Blend the peach pieces, sugar, and almond milk in a blender until smooth.
3. Pour the mixture into an ice cream maker and churn as per the manufacturer's instructions.
4. Once the gelato is thick and creamy, transfer it to a lidded container and freeze for at least 2 hours before serving.

**Calories:** Approx 140 kcal per serving (based on 6 servings)

## 43. Dragon Fruit Sorbet

**Ingredients:**

- 2 dragon fruits
- 150 grams of granulated sugar
- Juice of 1 lime

**Directions:**

1. Cut the dragon fruits in half, scoop out the flesh, and cut it into small pieces.
2. Blend the dragon fruit pieces, sugar, and lime juice in a blender until smooth.
3. Pour the mixture into an ice cream maker and churn according to the manufacturer's instructions.
4. Once the sorbet is of the desired consistency, transfer it to a lidded container and freeze for at least 2 hours before serving.

**Calories:** Approx 90 kcal per serving (based on 6 servings)

## 44. Strawberry-Banana Gelato

**Ingredients:**

- 250 grams of fresh strawberries
- 2 ripe bananas
- 200 grams of sugar
- 200 ml of almond milk

**Directions:**

1. Rinse the strawberries and pat them dry. Peel the bananas and cut them into slices.

2. Blend the strawberries, banana slices, sugar, and almond milk in a blender until smooth.
3. Pour the mixture into an ice cream maker and churn as per the manufacturer's instructions.
4. Once the gelato is thick and creamy, transfer it to a lidded container and freeze for at least 2 hours before serving.

**Calories:** Approx 180 kcal per serving (based on 6 servings)

# 45. Cucumber-Lime Sorbet

**Ingredients:**

- 2 large cucumbers
- 150 grams of granulated sugar
- Juice of 2 limes

**Directions:**

1. Peel the cucumbers, remove the seeds, and cut them into small pieces.
2. Blend the cucumber pieces, sugar, and lime juice in a blender until smooth.
3. Pour the mixture into an ice cream maker and churn according to the manufacturer's instructions.
4. Once the sorbet is of the desired consistency, transfer it to a lidded container and freeze for at least 2 hours before serving.

**Calories:** Approx 70 kcal per serving (based on 6 servings)

## 46. Passion Fruit Gelato II

**Ingredients:**

- Pulp of 10 passion fruits
- 200 grams of sugar
- 200 ml of coconut milk

**Directions:**

1. Scoop out the pulp of the passion fruits.
2. Blend the passion fruit pulp, sugar, and coconut milk in a blender until smooth.
3. Pour the mixture into an ice cream maker and churn as per the manufacturer's instructions.
4. Once the gelato is thick and creamy, transfer it to a lidded container and freeze for at least 2 hours before serving.

**Calories:** Approx 150 kcal per serving (based on 6 servings)

## 47. White Peach Sorbet

Ingredients:

- 4 white peaches
- 1 cup of sugar
- Juice of 1 lemon

Directions:

1. Slice the peaches and remove the pit. Blend until smooth.

2. Mix in the sugar and lemon juice, and blend again until well combined.
3. Pour the mixture into an ice cream maker and churn according to the manufacturer's instructions.
4. Transfer the sorbet to a lidded container and freeze for at least 2 hours before serving.

**Calories:** Approx 80 kcal per serving (based on 6 servings)

## 48. Fig and Honey Gelato

Ingredients:

- 8 fresh figs
- 1/4 cup of honey
- 1 cup of milk
- 1 cup of heavy cream

Directions:

1. Blend the figs and honey until smooth.
2. Add the milk and heavy cream and blend again.
3. Pour the mixture into an ice cream maker and churn according to the manufacturer's instructions.
4. Transfer the gelato to a lidded container and freeze for at least 4 hours before serving.

**Calories:** Approx 120 kcal per serving (based on 6 servings)

## 49. Tangerine Sorbet

Ingredients:

- Juice of 8 tangerines
- 1/2 cup sugar
- Zest of 1 tangerine

Directions:

1. In a saucepan, combine the tangerine juice, sugar, and zest. Cook over medium heat until the sugar has dissolved.
2. Remove from heat and let it cool.
3. Once cooled, pour the mixture into an ice cream maker and churn according to the manufacturer's instructions.
4. Transfer the sorbet to a lidded container and freeze for at least 2 hours before serving.

**Calories:** Approx 50 kcal per serving (based on 6 servings)

## 50. Cantaloupe Gelato

**Ingredients:**

- 1 medium cantaloupe
- 200 grams of sugar
- 200 ml of almond milk

**Directions:**

1. Cut the cantaloupe in half, remove the seeds, and cut it into small pieces.
2. Blend the cantaloupe pieces, sugar, and almond milk in a blender until smooth.
3. Pour the mixture into an ice cream maker and churn as per the manufacturer's instructions.
4. Once the gelato is thick and creamy, transfer it to a lidded container and freeze for at least 2 hours before serving.

**Calories:** Approx 120 kcal per serving (based on 6 servings)

## 51. Papaya Sorbet

**Ingredients:**

- 1 medium papaya
- 150 grams of granulated sugar
- Juice of 1 lime

**Directions:**

1. Peel the papaya, remove the seeds, and cut it into small pieces.
2. Blend the papaya pieces, sugar, and lime juice in a blender until smooth.
3. Pour the mixture into an ice cream maker and churn according to the manufacturer's instructions.
4. Once the sorbet is of the desired consistency, transfer it to a lidded container and freeze for at least 2 hours before serving.

**Calories:** Approx 90 kcal per serving (based on 6 servings)

## 52. Fig Gelato

**Ingredients:**

- 500 grams of fresh figs
- 200 grams of sugar
- 200 ml of almond milk

**Directions:**

1. Cut the figs in half and scoop out the flesh.
2. Blend the fig flesh, sugar, and almond milk in a blender until smooth.
3. Pour the mixture into an ice cream maker and churn as per the manufacturer's instructions.
4. Once the gelato is thick and creamy, transfer it to a lidded container and freeze for at least 2 hours before serving.

**Calories:** Approx 160 kcal per serving (based on 6 servings)

## 53. Honeydew Sorbet

**Ingredients:**

- 1 medium honeydew melon
- 150 grams of granulated sugar
- Juice of 1 lime

**Directions:**

1. Cut the honeydew melon in half, remove the seeds, and cut it into small pieces.
2. Blend the honeydew melon pieces, sugar, and lime juice in a blender until smooth.
3. Pour the mixture into an ice cream maker and churn according to the manufacturer's instructions.
4. Once the sorbet is of the desired consistency, transfer it to a lidded container and freeze for at least 2 hours before serving.

**Calories:** Approx 90 kcal per serving (based on 6 servings)

# 54. Apple Gelato

**Ingredients:**

- 4 medium apples
- 200 grams of sugar
- 200 ml of almond milk

**Directions:**

1. Peel the apples, remove the cores, and cut them into small pieces.
2. Blend the apple pieces, sugar, and almond milk in a blender until smooth.
3. Pour the mixture into an ice cream maker and churn as per the manufacturer's instructions.
4. Once the gelato is thick and creamy, transfer it to a lidded container and freeze for at least 2 hours before serving.

**Calories:** Approx 150 kcal per serving (based on 6 servings)

## 55. Cherry and Vanilla Gelato

Ingredients:

- 2 cups pitted cherries
- 1 cup sugar
- 1 cup whole milk
- 1 cup heavy cream
- 1 vanilla bean

Directions:

1. Blend the cherries until smooth and strain the juice to remove any solids.
2. In a saucepan, combine the cherry juice, sugar, milk, and heavy cream. Split the vanilla bean lengthwise, scrape out the seeds and add them to the saucepan.
3. Cook over medium heat until the sugar has dissolved.
4. Once cooled, pour the mixture into an ice cream maker and churn according to the manufacturer's instructions.
5. Transfer the gelato to a lidded container and freeze for at least 4 hours before serving.

**Calories:** Approx 130 kcal per serving (based on 6 servings)

## 56. Pomegranate Gelato

**Ingredients:**

- Seeds of 4 large pomegranates
- 200 grams of sugar
- 200 ml of almond milk

**Directions:**

1. Remove the seeds from the pomegranates.
2. Blend the pomegranate seeds, sugar, and almond milk in a blender until smooth. Strain the mixture to remove any remaining seed particles.
3. Pour the strained mixture into an ice cream maker and churn as per the manufacturer's instructions.
4. Once the gelato is thick and creamy, transfer it to a lidded container and freeze for at least 2 hours before serving.

**Calories:** Approx 170 kcal per serving (based on 6 servings)

# 57. Guava Gelato

Ingredients:

- 2 cups guava puree
- 1 cup sugar
- 1 1/2 cups whole milk
- 1/2 cup heavy cream

Directions:

1. In a saucepan, combine guava puree and sugar. Cook over medium heat until sugar is fully dissolved.
2. Remove from heat and let it cool.
3. Once cooled, mix in the milk and heavy cream.
4. Pour the mixture into an ice cream maker and churn according to the manufacturer's instructions.
5. Transfer the gelato to a lidded container and freeze for at least 4 hours before serving.

**Calories:** Approx 120

# 58. Kiwi Gelato

**Ingredients:**

- 6 ripe kiwis
- 200 grams of sugar
- 200 ml of almond milk

**Directions:**

1. Peel the kiwis and cut them into small pieces.
2. Blend the kiwi pieces, sugar, and almond milk in a blender until smooth.
3. Pour the mixture into an ice cream maker and churn as per the manufacturer's instructions.
4. Once the gelato is thick and creamy, transfer it to a lidded container and freeze for at least 2 hours before serving.

**Calories:** Approx 140 kcal per serving (based on 6 servings)

# 59. Mango Sorbet

**Ingredients:**

- 2 large mangoes
- 150 grams of granulated sugar
- Juice of 1 lime

**Directions:**

1. Peel the mangoes, remove the pits, and cut them into small pieces.

2. Blend the mango pieces, sugar, and lime juice in a blender until smooth.
3. Pour the mixture into an ice cream maker and churn according to the manufacturer's instructions.
4. Once the sorbet is of the desired consistency, transfer it to a lidded container and freeze for at least 2 hours before serving.

**Calories:** Approx 100 kcal per serving (based on 6 servings)

## 60. Cantaloupe Melon Sorbet

Ingredients:

- 1 medium cantaloupe melon
- 1/2 cup sugar
- Juice of 1 lemon

Directions:

1. Peel and dice the melon. Blend until smooth.
2. Mix in the sugar and lemon juice, and blend again until well combined.
3. Pour the mixture into an ice cream maker and churn according to the manufacturer's instructions.
4. Transfer the sorbet to a lidded container and freeze for at least 2 hours before serving.

**Calories:** Approx 60 kcal per serving (based on 6 servings)

# Chocolate Ice Cream

## 61. Classic Chocolate Gelato

**Ingredients:**

- 500 ml of whole milk
- 200 grams of sugar
- 200 grams of dark chocolate (70% cocoa)
- 4 egg yolks

**Directions:**

1. Chop the chocolate into small pieces and melt it over a double boiler or in the microwave.
2. In a saucepan, heat the milk until it's hot but not boiling.
3. In a separate bowl, beat the egg yolks and sugar until they're well combined.
4. Gradually add the hot milk into the egg yolk mixture, stirring continuously.
5. Pour the mixture back into the saucepan and cook over low heat until it thickens into a custard. Be careful not to let it boil.
6. Add the melted chocolate to the custard and stir until it's well incorporated.
7. Let the mixture cool down, then pour it into an ice cream maker. Churn as per the manufacturer's instructions.
8. Once the gelato is thick and creamy, transfer it to a lidded container and freeze for at least 2 hours before serving.

**Calories:** Approx 250 kcal per serving (based on 6 servings)

# 62. Chocolate Mint Gelato

**Ingredients:**

- 500 ml of whole milk
- 200 grams of sugar
- 200 grams of dark chocolate (70% cocoa)
- 4 egg yolks
- 2 teaspoons of peppermint extract

**Directions:**

1. Follow the same steps as the classic chocolate gelato recipe, but add the peppermint extract along with the melted chocolate.

**Calories:** Approx 250 kcal per serving (based on 6 servings)

# 63. Chocolate Orange Gelato

**Ingredients:**

- 500 ml of whole milk
- 200 grams of sugar
- 200 grams of dark chocolate (70% cocoa)
- 4 egg yolks
- Zest of 1 orange

**Directions:**

1. Follow the same steps as the classic chocolate gelato recipe, but add the orange zest along with the melted chocolate.

**Calories:** Approx 250 kcal per serving (based on 6 servings)

# 64. Mocha Gelato

### Ingredients:

- 500 ml of whole milk
- 200 grams of sugar
- 150 grams of dark chocolate (70% cocoa)
- 50 grams of instant coffee or espresso powder
- 4 egg yolks

### Directions:

1. Follow the same steps as the classic chocolate gelato recipe, but replace 50 grams of the chocolate with instant coffee or espresso powder.

**Calories:** Approx 230 kcal per serving (based on 6 servings)

# 65. Chocolate Chili Gelato

### Ingredients:

- 500 ml of whole milk
- 200 grams of sugar
- 200 grams of dark chocolate (70% cocoa)
- 4 egg yolks
- 1 teaspoon of chili powder

### Directions:

1. Follow the same steps as the classic chocolate gelato recipe, but add the chili powder along with the melted chocolate.

**Calories:** Approx 250 kcal per serving (based on 6 servings)

# 66. Chocolate Raspberry Swirl Gelato

**Ingredients:**

- 500 ml of whole milk
- 200 grams of sugar
- 200 grams of dark chocolate (70% cocoa)
- 4 egg yolks
- 150 grams of fresh raspberries
- 50 grams of sugar (for the raspberry sauce)

**Directions:**

1. Follow the same steps as the classic chocolate gelato recipe until it's churned and creamy.
2. Meanwhile, make a raspberry sauce by simmering the raspberries and 50 grams of sugar in a saucepan over low heat. Once it thickens, strain the sauce to remove the seeds, and let it cool.
3. As you transfer the churned gelato to a lidded container, layer it with the cooled raspberry sauce to create a swirl effect. Freeze for at least 2 hours before serving.

**Calories:** Approx 280 kcal per serving (based on 6 servings)

# 67. Chocolate Coconut Gelato

**Ingredients:**

- 400 ml of whole milk
- 100 ml of coconut milk
- 200 grams of sugar

- 200 grams of dark chocolate (70% cocoa)
- 4 egg yolks

**Directions:**

1. Follow the same steps as the classic chocolate gelato recipe, but replace 100 ml of whole milk with coconut milk.

**Calories:** Approx 260 kcal per serving (based on 6 servings)

# 68. Chocolate Hazelnut Gelato

**Ingredients:**

- 500 ml of whole milk
- 200 grams of sugar
- 150 grams of dark chocolate (70% cocoa)
- 50 grams of hazelnut paste
- 4 egg yolks

**Directions:**

1. Follow the same steps as the classic chocolate gelato recipe, but replace 50 grams of the chocolate with hazelnut paste.

**Calories:** Approx 270 kcal per serving (based on 6 servings)

# 69. Chocolate Peanut Butter Gelato

**Ingredients:**

- 500 ml of whole milk
- 200 grams of sugar
- 150 grams of dark chocolate (70% cocoa)

- 50 grams of smooth peanut butter
- 4 egg yolks

**Directions:**

1. Follow the same steps as the classic chocolate gelato recipe, but replace 50 grams of the chocolate with smooth peanut butter.

**Calories:** Approx 280 kcal per serving (based on 6 servings)

# 70. Chocolate Banana Gelato

**Ingredients:**

- 400 ml of whole milk
- 100 ml of mashed ripe banana
- 200 grams of sugar
- 200 grams of dark chocolate (70% cocoa)
- 4 egg yolks

**Directions:**

1. Follow the same steps as the classic chocolate gelato recipe, but replace 100 ml of whole milk with mashed ripe banana.

**Calories:** Approx 260 kcal per serving (based on 6 servings)

# 71. Chocolate Avocado Gelato

**Ingredients:**

- 400 ml of whole milk
- 100 ml of ripe avocado, mashed
- 200 grams of sugar

- 200 grams of dark chocolate (70% cocoa)
- 4 egg yolks

**Directions:**

1. Follow the same steps as the classic chocolate gelato recipe, but replace 100 ml of whole milk with mashed ripe avocado.

**Calories:** Approx 260 kcal per serving (based on 6 servings)

# 72. Salted Caramel Chocolate Gelato

**Ingredients:**

- 500 ml of whole milk
- 200 grams of sugar
- 200 grams of dark chocolate (70% cocoa)
- 4 egg yolks
- 100 grams of caramel sauce
- 1 teaspoon of sea salt

**Directions:**

1. Follow the same steps as the classic chocolate gelato recipe.
2. Once the gelato is churned and creamy, add the caramel sauce and sea salt, and mix until well incorporated. Freeze for at least 2 hours before serving.

**Calories:** Approx 280 kcal per serving (based on 6 servings)

## 73. Chocolate Almond Gelato

**Ingredients:**

- 500 ml of whole milk
- 200 grams of sugar
- 150 grams of dark chocolate (70% cocoa)
- 50 grams of almond paste
- 4 egg yolks

**Directions:**

1. Follow the same steps as the classic chocolate gelato recipe, but replace 50 grams of the chocolate with almond paste.

**Calories:** Approx 260 kcal per serving (based on 6 servings)

## 74. Chocolate Amaretto Gelato

**Ingredients:**

- 500 ml of whole milk
- 200 grams of sugar
- 200 grams of dark chocolate (70% cocoa)
- 4 egg yolks
- 3 tablespoons of Amaretto liqueur

**Directions:**

1. Follow the same steps as the classic chocolate gelato recipe, but add the Amaretto liqueur just before you start churning the mixture in the ice cream maker.

**Calories:** Approx 260 kcal per serving (based on 6 servings)

## 75. Chocolate Cherry Gelato

**Ingredients:**

- 500 ml of whole milk
- 200 grams of sugar
- 200 grams of dark chocolate (70% cocoa)
- 4 egg yolks
- 100 grams of pitted cherries, chopped

**Directions:**

1. Follow the same steps as the classic chocolate gelato recipe.
2. Once the gelato is churned and creamy, add the chopped cherries and mix until well incorporated. Freeze for at least 2 hours before serving.

**Calories:** Approx 260 kcal per serving (based on 6 servings)

## 76. Chocolate Pistachio Gelato

**Ingredients:**

- 500 ml of whole milk
- 200 grams of sugar
- 150 grams of dark chocolate (70% cocoa)
- 50 grams of pistachio paste
- 4 egg yolks

**Directions:**

1. Follow the same steps as the classic chocolate gelato recipe, but replace 50 grams of the chocolate with pistachio paste.

**Calories:** Approx 270 kcal per serving (based on 6 servings)

## 77. Chocolate Marshmallow Gelato

**Ingredients:**

- 500 ml of whole milk
- 200 grams of sugar
- 200 grams of dark chocolate (70% cocoa)
- 4 egg yolks
- 100 grams of mini marshmallows

**Directions:**

1. Follow the same steps as the classic chocolate gelato recipe.
2. Once the gelato is churned and creamy, add the mini marshmallows and mix until well incorporated. Freeze for at least 2 hours before serving.

**Calories:** Approx 280 kcal per serving (based on 6 servings)

## 78. Chocolate Tiramisu Gelato

**Ingredients:**

- 500 ml of whole milk
- 200 grams of sugar
- 200 grams of dark chocolate (70% cocoa)
- 4 egg yolks

- 50 grams of espresso powder
- 50 grams of ladyfingers, crushed
- 2 tablespoons of Marsala wine

**Directions:**

1. Follow the same steps as the classic chocolate gelato recipe, but add the espresso powder along with the chocolate.
2. Once the gelato is churned and creamy, add the crushed ladyfingers and Marsala wine, and mix until well incorporated. Freeze for at least 2 hours before serving.

**Calories:** Approx 280 kcal per serving (based on 6 servings)

# 79. Chocolate Blueberry Gelato

**Ingredients:**

- 500 ml of whole milk
- 200 grams of sugar
- 200 grams of dark chocolate (70% cocoa)
- 4 egg yolks
- 100 grams of blueberries, crushed

**Directions:**

1. Follow the same steps as the classic chocolate gelato recipe.
2. Once the gelato is churned and creamy, add the crushed blueberries and mix until well incorporated. Freeze for at least 2 hours before serving.

**Calories:** Approx 260 kcal per serving (based on 6 servings)

# 80. Chocolate Cookie Gelato

**Ingredients:**

- 500 ml of whole milk
- 200 grams of sugar
- 200 grams of dark chocolate (70% cocoa)
- 4 egg yolks
- 100 grams of cookies, crushed

**Directions:**

1. Follow the same steps as the classic chocolate gelato recipe.
2. Once the gelato is churned and creamy, add the crushed cookies and mix until well incorporated. Freeze for at least 2 hours before serving.

**Calories:** Approx 280 kcal per serving (based on 6 servings)

# 81. Chocolate Pecan Gelato

**Ingredients:**

- 500 ml of whole milk
- 200 grams of sugar
- 200 grams of dark chocolate (70% cocoa)
- 4 egg yolks
- 100 grams of pecans, chopped and toasted

**Directions:**

1. Follow the same steps as the classic chocolate gelato recipe.

2. Once the gelato is churned and creamy, add the chopped pecans and mix until well incorporated. Freeze for at least 2 hours before serving.

**Calories:** Approx 280 kcal per serving (based on 6 servings)

# 82. Chocolate Caramel Swirl Gelato

**Ingredients:**

- 500 ml of whole milk
- 200 grams of sugar
- 200 grams of dark chocolate (70% cocoa)
- 4 egg yolks
- 100 grams of caramel sauce

**Directions:**

1. Follow the same steps as the classic chocolate gelato recipe.
2. As you transfer the churned gelato to a lidded container, layer it with caramel sauce to create a swirl effect. Freeze for at least 2 hours before serving.

**Calories:** Approx 280 kcal per serving (based on 6 servings)

# 83. Chocolate and Toasted Almond Gelato

**Ingredients:**

- 500 ml of whole milk
- 200 grams of sugar
- 200 grams of dark chocolate (70% cocoa)

- 4 egg yolks
- 100 grams of almonds, chopped and toasted

**Directions:**

1. Follow the same steps as the classic chocolate gelato recipe.
2. Once the gelato is churned and creamy, add the chopped and toasted almonds, mixing until well incorporated. Freeze for at least 2 hours before serving.

**Calories:** Approx 280 kcal per serving (based on 6 servings)

# 84. Chocolate Macadamia Gelato

**Ingredients:**

- 500 ml of whole milk
- 200 grams of sugar
- 200 grams of dark chocolate (70% cocoa)
- 4 egg yolks
- 100 grams of macadamia nuts, chopped

**Directions:**

1. Follow the same steps as the classic chocolate gelato recipe.
2. Once the gelato is churned and creamy, add the chopped macadamia nuts and mix until well incorporated. Freeze for at least 2 hours before serving.

**Calories:** Approx 280 kcal per serving (based on 6 servings)

## 85. Chocolate and Candied Orange Peel Gelato

**Ingredients:**

- 500 ml of whole milk
- 200 grams of sugar
- 200 grams of dark chocolate (70% cocoa)
- 4 egg yolks
- 100 grams of candied orange peel, chopped

**Directions:**

1. Follow the same steps as the classic chocolate gelato recipe.
2. Once the gelato is churned and creamy, add the chopped candied orange peel and mix until well incorporated. Freeze for at least 2 hours before serving.

**Calories:** Approx 280 kcal per serving (based on 6 servings)

## 86. Dark Chocolate and Mint Gelato

**Ingredients:**

- 500 ml of whole milk
- 200 grams of sugar
- 200 grams of dark chocolate (70% cocoa)
- 4 egg yolks
- 2 tablespoons of fresh mint, finely chopped

**Directions:**

1. Follow the same steps as the classic chocolate gelato recipe.

2. Once the gelato is churned and creamy, add the finely chopped mint and mix until well incorporated. Freeze for at least 2 hours before serving.

**Calories:** Approx 270 kcal per serving (based on 6 servings)

# 87. Chocolate and Roasted Cashew Gelato

**Ingredients:**

- 500 ml of whole milk
- 200 grams of sugar
- 200 grams of dark chocolate (70% cocoa)
- 4 egg yolks
- 100 grams of cashews, roasted and chopped

**Directions:**

1. Follow the same steps as the classic chocolate gelato recipe.
2. Once the gelato is churned and creamy, add the chopped roasted cashews and mix until well incorporated. Freeze for at least 2 hours before serving.

**Calories:** Approx 280 kcal per serving (based on 6 servings)

# 88. Chocolate and Ginger Gelato

**Ingredients:**

- 500 ml of whole milk
- 200 grams of sugar
- 200 grams of dark chocolate (70% cocoa)

- 4 egg yolks
- 1 tablespoon of fresh ginger, grated

**Directions:**

1. Follow the same steps as the classic chocolate gelato recipe, but add the grated ginger along with the chocolate.

**Calories:** Approx 270 kcal per serving (based on 6 servings)

# 89. Chocolate and Raisin Gelato

**Ingredients:**

- 500 ml of whole milk
- 200 grams of sugar
- 200 grams of dark chocolate (70% cocoa)
- 4 egg yolks
- 100 grams of raisins, soaked in warm water and drained

**Directions:**

1. Follow the same steps as the classic chocolate gelato recipe.
2. Once the gelato is churned and creamy, add the drained raisins and mix until well incorporated. Freeze for at least 2 hours before serving.

**Calories:** Approx 270 kcal per serving (based on 6 servings)

# 90. Chocolate and Mocha Gelato

**Ingredients:**

- 500 ml of whole milk
- 200 grams of sugar
- 200 grams of dark chocolate (70% cocoa)
- 4 egg yolks
- 2 tablespoons of instant coffee

**Directions:**

1. Follow the same steps as the classic chocolate gelato recipe, but add the instant coffee along with the chocolate.

**Calories:** Approx 270 kcal per serving (based on 6 servings)

# 91. Chocolate and Coconut Gelato

**Ingredients:**

- 500 ml of whole milk
- 200 grams of sugar
- 200 grams of dark chocolate (70% cocoa)
- 4 egg yolks
- 100 grams of shredded coconut

**Directions:**

1. Follow the same steps as the classic chocolate gelato recipe.

2. Once the gelato is churned and creamy, add the shredded coconut and mix until well incorporated. Freeze for at least 2 hours before serving.

**Calories:** Approx 280 kcal per serving (based on 6 servings)

# 92. Chocolate Banana Gelato II

**Ingredients:**

- 500 ml of whole milk
- 200 grams of sugar
- 200 grams of dark chocolate (70% cocoa)
- 4 egg yolks
- 2 ripe bananas, mashed

**Directions:**

1. Follow the same steps as the classic chocolate gelato recipe.
2. Once the gelato is churned and creamy, add the mashed bananas and mix until well incorporated. Freeze for at least 2 hours before serving.

**Calories:** Approx 290 kcal per serving (based on 6 servings)

# 93. Chocolate and Caramelized Hazelnut Gelato

**Ingredients:**

- 500 ml of whole milk
- 200 grams of sugar
- 200 grams of dark chocolate (70% cocoa)

- 4 egg yolks
- 100 grams of hazelnuts, caramelized and chopped

**Directions:**

1. Follow the same steps as the classic chocolate gelato recipe.
2. Once the gelato is churned and creamy, add the chopped caramelized hazelnuts and mix until well incorporated. Freeze for at least 2 hours before serving.

**Calories:** Approx 290 kcal per serving (based on 6 servings)

# 94. Chocolate and Honeycomb Gelato

**Ingredients:**

- 500 ml of whole milk
- 200 grams of sugar
- 200 grams of dark chocolate (70% cocoa)
- 4 egg yolks
- 100 grams of honeycomb, crushed

**Directions:**

1. Follow the same steps as the classic chocolate gelato recipe.
2. Once the gelato is churned and creamy, add the crushed honeycomb and mix until well incorporated. Freeze for at least 2 hours before serving.

**Calories:** Approx 290 kcal per serving (based on 6 servings)

# 95. Chocolate and Chili Gelato

**Ingredients:**

- 500 ml of whole milk
- 200 grams of sugar
- 200 grams of dark chocolate (70% cocoa)
- 4 egg yolks
- 1 teaspoon of chili powder

**Directions:**

1. Follow the same steps as the classic chocolate gelato recipe, but add the chili powder along with the chocolate.

**Calories:** Approx 270 kcal per serving (based on 6 servings)

# 96. Chocolate and Raspberry Gelato

**Ingredients:**

- 500 ml of whole milk
- 200 grams of sugar
- 200 grams of dark chocolate (70% cocoa)
- 4 egg yolks
- 200 grams of fresh raspberries, crushed

**Directions:**

1. Follow the same steps as the classic chocolate gelato recipe.

2. Once the gelato is churned and creamy, add the crushed raspberries and mix until well incorporated. Freeze for at least 2 hours before serving.

**Calories:** Approx 290 kcal per serving (based on 6 servings)

# 97. Chocolate and Candied Ginger Gelato

**Ingredients:**

- 500 ml of whole milk
- 200 grams of sugar
- 200 grams of dark chocolate (70% cocoa)
- 4 egg yolks
- 100 grams of candied ginger, chopped

**Directions:**

1. Follow the same steps as the classic chocolate gelato recipe.
2. Once the gelato is churned and creamy, add the chopped candied ginger and mix until well incorporated. Freeze for at least 2 hours before serving.

**Calories:** Approx 290 kcal per serving (based on 6 servings)

# 98. Chocolate and Walnut Gelato

**Ingredients:**

- 500 ml of whole milk
- 200 grams of sugar
- 200 grams of dark chocolate (70% cocoa)

- 4 egg yolks
- 100 grams of walnuts, chopped

**Directions:**

1. Follow the same steps as the classic chocolate gelato recipe.
2. Once the gelato is churned and creamy, add the chopped walnuts and mix until well incorporated. Freeze for at least 2 hours before serving.

**Calories:** Approx 290 kcal per serving (based on 6 servings)

# 99. Chocolate and Bourbon Gelato

**Ingredients:**

- 500 ml of whole milk
- 200 grams of sugar
- 200 grams of dark chocolate (70% cocoa)
- 4 egg yolks
- 2 tablespoons of bourbon

**Directions:**

1. Follow the same steps as the classic chocolate gelato recipe.
2. Once the gelato is churned and creamy, add the bourbon and mix until well incorporated. Freeze for at least 2 hours before serving.

**Calories:** Approx 270 kcal per serving (based on 6 servings)

# 100. Chocolate and Salted Caramel Gelato

**Ingredients:**

- 500 ml of whole milk
- 200 grams of sugar
- 200 grams of dark chocolate (70% cocoa)
- 4 egg yolks
- 100 grams of salted caramel sauce

**Directions:**

1. Follow the same steps as the classic chocolate gelato recipe.
2. As you transfer the churned gelato to a lidded container, layer it with the salted caramel sauce to create a swirl effect. Freeze for at least 2 hours before serving.

**Calories:** Approx 290 kcal per serving (based on 6 servings)

# Coffee Ice Cream

## 101. Classic Coffee Gelato

**Ingredients:**

- 500 ml of whole milk
- 200 grams of sugar
- 2 tablespoons of instant coffee
- 4 egg yolks

**Directions:**

1. In a medium-sized pot, mix the milk and instant coffee. Heat until hot, but not boiling.
2. In a separate bowl, beat the egg yolks and sugar until pale and creamy.
3. Gradually pour the hot milk into the egg yolk mixture, stirring constantly.
4. Return the mixture to the pot and heat gently, stirring continuously, until it coats the back of a spoon.
5. Remove from heat and let the mixture cool down, then refrigerate for at least 2 hours.
6. Once the mixture is thoroughly chilled, churn it in an ice cream maker according to the manufacturer's instructions.

**Nutritional values:** Approx 200 kcal per serving (based on 6 servings), 6g protein, 30g carbohydrates, 7g fat

# 102. Coffee and Cinnamon Gelato

**Ingredients:**

- 500 ml of whole milk
- 200 grams of sugar
- 2 tablespoons of instant coffee
- 4 egg yolks
- 1 teaspoon of ground cinnamon

**Directions:**

1. Follow the same steps as the classic coffee gelato recipe, but add the ground cinnamon along with the instant coffee.

**Nutritional values:** Approx 205 kcal per serving (based on 6 servings), 6g protein, 31g carbohydrates, 7g fat

# 103. Coffee and Vanilla Gelato

**Ingredients:**

- 500 ml of whole milk
- 200 grams of sugar
- 2 tablespoons of instant coffee
- 4 egg yolks
- 1 vanilla bean, seeds scraped

**Directions:**

1. Follow the same steps as the classic coffee gelato recipe, but add the vanilla seeds along with the instant coffee.

**Nutritional values:** Approx 210 kcal per serving (based on 6 servings), 6g protein, 31g carbohydrates, 7g fat

# 104. Coffee and Hazelnut Gelato

**Ingredients:**

- 500 ml of whole milk
- 200 grams of sugar
- 2 tablespoons of instant coffee
- 4 egg yolks
- 100 grams of hazelnuts, toasted and chopped

**Directions:**

1. Follow the same steps as the classic coffee gelato recipe.
2. Once the gelato is churned and creamy, add the toasted hazelnuts and mix until well incorporated. Freeze for at least 2 hours before serving.

**Nutritional values:** Approx 240 kcal per serving (based on 6 servings), 7g protein, 31g carbohydrates, 12g fat

# 105. Coffee and Caramel Gelato

**Ingredients:**

- 500 ml of whole milk
- 200 grams of sugar
- 2 tablespoons of instant coffee
- 4 egg yolks
- 100 grams of caramel sauce

**Directions:**

1. Follow the same steps as the classic coffee gelato recipe.
2. As you transfer the churned gelato to a lidded container, layer it with caramel sauce to create a swirl effect. Freeze for at least 2 hours before serving.

**Nutritional values:** Approx 240 kcal per serving (based on 6 servings), 6g protein, 38g carbohydrates, 8g fat

# 106. Coffee and Chocolate Chip Gelato

**Ingredients:**

- 500 ml of whole milk
- 200 grams of sugar
- 2 tablespoons of instant coffee
- 4 egg yolks
- 100 grams of mini chocolate chips

**Directions:**

1. Follow the same steps as the classic coffee gelato recipe.
2. Once the gelato is churned and creamy, add the mini chocolate chips and mix until well incorporated. Freeze for at least 2 hours before serving.

**Nutritional values:** Approx 250 kcal per serving (based on 6 servings), 6g protein, 32g carbohydrates, 11g fat

# 107. Coffee and Almond Gelato

**Ingredients:**

- 500 ml of whole milk
- 200 grams of sugar

- 2 tablespoons of instant coffee
- 4 egg yolks
- 100 grams of almonds, toasted and chopped

**Directions:**

1. Follow the same steps as the classic coffee gelato recipe.
2. Once the gelato is churned and creamy, add the toasted almonds and mix until well incorporated. Freeze for at least 2 hours before serving.

**Nutritional values:** Approx 240 kcal per serving (based on 6 servings), 7g protein, 31g carbohydrates, 12g fat

# 108. Coffee and Coconut Gelato

**Ingredients:**

- 500 ml of whole milk
- 200 grams of sugar
- 2 tablespoons of instant coffee
- 4 egg yolks
- 100 grams of shredded coconut

**Directions:**

1. Follow the same steps as the classic coffee gelato recipe.
2. Once the gelato is churned and creamy, add the shredded coconut and mix until well incorporated. Freeze for at least 2 hours before serving.

**Nutritional values:** Approx 230 kcal per serving (based on 6 servings), 6g protein, 32g carbohydrates, 10g fat

# 109. Coffee and Irish Cream Gelato

**Ingredients:**

- 500 ml of whole milk
- 200 grams of sugar
- 2 tablespoons of instant coffee
- 4 egg yolks
- 2 tablespoons of Irish cream liqueur

**Directions:**

1. Follow the same steps as the classic coffee gelato recipe.
2. Once the gelato is churned and creamy, add the Irish cream liqueur and mix until well incorporated. Freeze for at least 2 hours before serving.

**Nutritional values:** Approx 210 kcal per serving (based on 6 servings), 6g protein, 31g carbohydrates, 7g fat

# 110. Coffee and Whiskey Gelato

**Ingredients:**

- 500 ml of whole milk
- 200 grams of sugar
- 2 tablespoons of instant coffee
- 4 egg yolks
- 2 tablespoons of whiskey

**Directions:**

1. Follow the same steps as the classic coffee gelato recipe.

2. Once the gelato is churned and creamy, add the whiskey and mix until well incorporated. Freeze for at least 2 hours before serving.

**Nutritional values:** Approx 210 kcal per serving (based on 6 servings), 6g protein, 31g carbohydrates, 7g fat

# 111. Coffee and Toffee Gelato

**Ingredients:**

- 500 ml of whole milk
- 200 grams of sugar
- 2 tablespoons of instant coffee
- 4 egg yolks
- 100 grams of toffee pieces

**Directions:**

1. Follow the same steps as the classic coffee gelato recipe.
2. Once the gelato is churned and creamy, add the toffee pieces and mix until well incorporated. Freeze for at least 2 hours before serving.

**Nutritional values:** Approx 250 kcal per serving (based on 6 servings), 6g protein, 36g carbohydrates, 10g fat

# 112. Coffee and Banana Gelato

**Ingredients:**

- 500 ml of whole milk
- 200 grams of sugar
- 2 tablespoons of instant coffee

- 4 egg yolks
- 2 ripe bananas, mashed

**Directions:**

1. Follow the same steps as the classic coffee gelato recipe.
2. Once the gelato is churned and creamy, add the mashed bananas and mix until well incorporated. Freeze for at least 2 hours before serving.

**Nutritional values:** Approx 225 kcal per serving (based on 6 servings), 6g protein, 35g carbohydrates, 7g fat

# 113. Coffee and Cardamom Gelato

**Ingredients:**

- 500 ml of whole milk
- 200 grams of sugar
- 2 tablespoons of instant coffee
- 4 egg yolks
- 1 teaspoon of ground cardamom

**Directions:**

1. Follow the same steps as the classic coffee gelato recipe, but add the ground cardamom along with the instant coffee.

**Nutritional values:** Approx 205 kcal per serving (based on 6 servings), 6g protein, 31g carbohydrates, 7g fat

## 114. Coffee and Pistachio Gelato

**Ingredients:**

- 500 ml of whole milk
- 200 grams of sugar
- 2 tablespoons of instant coffee
- 4 egg yolks
- 100 grams of pistachios, chopped

**Directions:**

1. Follow the same steps as the classic coffee gelato recipe.
2. Once the gelato is churned and creamy, add the chopped pistachios and mix until well incorporated. Freeze for at least 2 hours before serving.

**Nutritional values:** Approx 240 kcal per serving (based on 6 servings), 7g protein, 31g carbohydrates, 12g fat

## 115. Coffee and Cherry Gelato

**Ingredients:**

- 500 ml of whole milk
- 200 grams of sugar
- 2 tablespoons of instant coffee
- 4 egg yolks
- 200 grams of cherries, pitted and chopped

**Directions:**

1. Follow the same steps as the classic coffee gelato recipe.
2. Once the gelato is churned and creamy, add the chopped cherries and mix until well incorporated. Freeze for at least 2 hours before serving.

**Nutritional values:** Approx 210 kcal per serving (based on 6 servings), 6g protein, 33g carbohydrates, 7g fat

# 116. Coffee and Rum Gelato

**Ingredients:**

- 500 ml of whole milk
- 200 grams of sugar
- 2 tablespoons of instant coffee
- 4 egg yolks
- 2 tablespoons of rum

**Directions:**

1. Follow the same steps as the classic coffee gelato recipe.
2. Once the gelato is churned and creamy, add the rum and mix until well incorporated. Freeze for at least 2 hours before serving.

**Nutritional values:** Approx 210 kcal per serving (based on 6 servings), 6g protein, 31g carbohydrates, 7g fat

# 117. Coffee and Peppermint Gelato

**Ingredients:**

- 500 ml of whole milk
- 200 grams of sugar

- 2 tablespoons of instant coffee
- 4 egg yolks
- 2 teaspoons of peppermint extract

**Directions:**

1. Follow the same steps as the classic coffee gelato recipe.
2. Once the gelato is churned and creamy, add the peppermint extract and mix until well incorporated. Freeze for at least 2 hours before serving.

**Nutritional values:** Approx 200 kcal per serving (based on 6 servings), 6g protein, 30g carbohydrates, 7g fat

# 118. Coffee and Peanut Butter Gelato

**Ingredients:**

- 500 ml of whole milk
- 200 grams of sugar
- 2 tablespoons of instant coffee
- 4 egg yolks
- 100 grams of peanut butter

**Directions:**

1. Follow the same steps as the classic coffee gelato recipe.
2. Once the gelato is churned and creamy, add the peanut butter and mix until well incorporated. Freeze for at least 2 hours before serving.

**Nutritional values:** Approx 260 kcal per serving (based on 6 servings), 8g protein, 32g carbohydrates, 14g fat

## 119. Coffee and Maple Syrup Gelato

**Ingredients:**

- 500 ml of whole milk
- 200 grams of sugar
- 2 tablespoons of instant coffee
- 4 egg yolks
- 50 ml of maple syrup

**Directions:**

1. Follow the same steps as the classic coffee gelato recipe.
2. Once the gelato is churned and creamy, add the maple syrup and mix until well incorporated. Freeze for at least 2 hours before serving.

**Nutritional values:** Approx 220 kcal per serving (based on 6 servings), 6g protein, 33g carbohydrates, 7g fat

## 120. Coffee and Oreo Gelato

**Ingredients:**

- 500 ml of whole milk
- 200 grams of sugar
- 2 tablespoons of instant coffee
- 4 egg yolks
- 100 grams of Oreo cookies, crushed

**Directions:**

1. Follow the same steps as the classic coffee gelato recipe.

2. Once the gelato is churned and creamy, add the crushed Oreo cookies and mix until well incorporated. Freeze for at least 2 hours before serving.

**Nutritional values:** Approx 250 kcal per serving (based on 6 servings), 6g protein, 36g carbohydrates, 10g fat

# 121. Classic Coffee Ice Cream

Ingredients:

- 1 cup whole milk
- 3/4 cup sugar
- 2 cups heavy cream
- 2 tablespoons instant coffee granules

Directions:

1. In a medium saucepan, mix together milk and sugar until the sugar is dissolved.
2. Stir in the heavy cream and instant coffee.
3. Cook the mixture over medium heat until it begins to steam.
4. Remove from heat and let it cool.
5. Once cooled, pour the mixture into an ice cream maker and churn according to the manufacturer's instructions.
6. Transfer the ice cream to a lidded container and freeze for at least 4 hours before serving.

**Nutritional values:** Approx 220 kcal per serving (based on 6 servings), 2g protein, 15g carbohydrates, 16g fat

# 122. Vegan Coffee Coconut Milk Ice Cream

Ingredients:

- 2 cans of full-fat coconut milk
- 1/2 cup of agave syrup
- 1/4 cup of instant coffee granules

Directions:

1. Blend together the coconut milk, agave syrup, and coffee in a blender until smooth.
2. Pour the mixture into an ice cream maker and churn according to the manufacturer's instructions.
3. Transfer the ice cream to a lidded container and freeze for at least 4 hours before serving.

**Nutritional values:** Approx 180 kcal per serving (based on 6 servings), 1g protein, 12g carbohydrates, 14g fat

# 123. Mocha Chip Ice Cream

Ingredients:

- 1 cup whole milk
- 2 cups heavy cream
- 3/4 cup sugar
- 2 tablespoons instant coffee granules
- 1/2 cup mini chocolate chips

Directions:

1. In a medium saucepan, mix together milk and sugar until the sugar is dissolved.
2. Stir in the heavy cream and instant coffee.
3. Cook the mixture over medium heat until it begins to steam.
4. Remove from heat, let it cool and stir in the mini chocolate chips.
5. Once cooled, pour the mixture into an ice cream maker and churn according to the manufacturer's instructions.
6. Transfer the ice cream to a lidded container and freeze for at least 4 hours before serving.

**Nutritional values:** Approx 240 kcal per serving (based on 6 servings), 3g protein, 20g carbohydrates, 16g fat

# 124. Coffee and Coconut Milk Gelato

**Ingredients:**

- 500 ml of coconut milk
- 200 grams of sugar
- 2 tablespoons of instant coffee
- 4 egg yolks

**Directions:**

1. Heat the coconut milk over medium heat until it just begins to simmer. Don't let it boil.
2. In a separate bowl, mix the egg yolks and sugar until they become light and creamy.
3. Dissolve the instant coffee in a small amount of hot water and add to the egg yolk mixture.

4. Slowly pour the hot coconut milk into the egg yolk mixture while continuing to stir. Mix until everything is well incorporated.
5. Return the mixture to the heat and cook on low until it thickens enough to coat the back of a spoon. Don't let it boil.
6. Remove from heat and let it cool. Once cooled, place it in the refrigerator for at least 2 hours or overnight.
7. Churn the mixture in an ice cream maker according to the manufacturer's instructions.
8. Transfer the gelato to a lidded container and freeze for at least 2 hours before serving.

**Nutritional values:** Approx 220 kcal per serving (based on 6 servings), 5g protein, 31g carbohydrates, 11g fat

# 125. Coffee and Marshmallow Gelato

**Ingredients:**

- 500 ml of whole milk
- 200 grams of sugar
- 2 tablespoons of instant coffee
- 4 egg yolks
- 100 grams of mini marshmallows

**Directions:**

1. Follow the same steps as the classic coffee gelato recipe.
2. Once the gelato is churned and creamy, add the mini marshmallows and mix until well incorporated. Freeze for at least 2 hours before serving.

**Nutritional values:** Approx 230 kcal per serving (based on 6 servings), 6g protein, 35g carbohydrates, 7g fat

## 126. Iced Coffee Sorbet

Ingredients:

- 4 cups strong brewed coffee
- 1 cup white sugar
- 1 teaspoon vanilla extract

Directions:

1. Combine the coffee and sugar in a medium saucepan and bring to a boil over medium heat, stirring until the sugar is completely dissolved.
2. Remove from heat and stir in the vanilla extract.
3. Let the mixture cool, then refrigerate until chilled.
4. Once chilled, churn the mixture in an ice cream maker according to the manufacturer's instructions.
5. Transfer the sorbet to a lidded container and freeze for at least 4 hours before serving.

**Nutritional values:** Approx 60 kcal per serving (based on 6 servings), 0g protein, 15g carbohydrates, 1g fat

## 127. Coffee and Dark Chocolate Chip Gelato

**Ingredients:**

- 500 ml of whole milk
- 200 grams of sugar
- 2 tablespoons of instant coffee

- 4 egg yolks
- 100 grams of dark chocolate chips

**Directions:**

1. Follow the same steps as the classic coffee gelato recipe.
2. Once the gelato is churned and creamy, add the dark chocolate chips and mix until well incorporated. Freeze for at least 2 hours before serving.

**Nutritional values:** Approx 250 kcal per serving (based on 6 servings), 7g protein, 31g carbohydrates, 12g fat

# 128. Coffee and Macadamia Nut Gelato

**Ingredients:**

- 500 ml of whole milk
- 200 grams of sugar
- 2 tablespoons of instant coffee
- 4 egg yolks
- 100 grams of macadamia nuts, chopped

**Directions:**

1. Follow the same steps as the classic coffee gelato recipe.
2. Once the gelato is churned and creamy, add the chopped macadamia nuts and mix until well incorporated. Freeze for at least 2 hours before serving.

**Nutritional values:** Approx 250 kcal per serving (based on 6 servings), 7g protein, 31g carbohydrates, 15g fat

# 129. Coffee and Amaretto Gelato

**Ingredients:**

- 500 ml of whole milk
- 200 grams of sugar
- 2 tablespoons of instant coffee
- 4 egg yolks
- 2 tablespoons of Amaretto liqueur

**Directions:**

1. Follow the same steps as the classic coffee gelato recipe.
2. Once the gelato is churned and creamy, add the Amaretto liqueur and mix until well incorporated. Freeze for at least 2 hours before serving.

**Nutritional values:** Approx 210 kcal per serving (based on 6 servings), 6g protein, 31g carbohydrates, 7g fat

# 130. Coffee and Honey Gelato

**Ingredients:**

- 500 ml of whole milk
- 200 grams of sugar
- 2 tablespoons of instant coffee
- 4 egg yolks
- 2 tablespoons of honey

**Directions:**

1. Follow the same steps as the classic coffee gelato recipe.

2. Once the gelato is churned and creamy, add the honey and mix until well incorporated. Freeze for at least 2 hours before serving.

**Nutritional values:** Approx 210 kcal per serving (based on 6 servings), 6g protein, 33g carbohydrates, 7g fat

# 131. Coffee and Bourbon Gelato

**Ingredients:**

- 500 ml of whole milk
- 200 grams of sugar
- 2 tablespoons of instant coffee
- 4 egg yolks
- 2 tablespoons of bourbon

**Directions:**

1. Follow the same steps as the classic coffee gelato recipe.
2. Once the gelato is churned and creamy, add the bourbon and mix until well incorporated. Freeze for at least 2 hours before serving.

**Nutritional values:** Approx 210 kcal per serving (based on 6 servings), 6g protein, 31g carbohydrates, 7g fat

# 132. Coffee and Mint Chocolate Chip Gelato

**Ingredients:**

- 500 ml of whole milk

- 200 grams of sugar
- 2 tablespoons of instant coffee
- 4 egg yolks
- 100 grams of mint chocolate chips

**Directions:**

1. Follow the same steps as the classic coffee gelato recipe.
2. Once the gelato is churned and creamy, add the mint chocolate chips and mix until well incorporated. Freeze for at least 2 hours before serving.

**Nutritional values:** Approx 250 kcal per serving (based on 6 servings), 7g protein, 32g carbohydrates, 12g fat

# 133. Coffee and Pecan Gelato

**Ingredients:**

- 500 ml of whole milk
- 200 grams of sugar
- 2 tablespoons of instant coffee
- 4 egg yolks
- 100 grams of pecans, chopped

**Directions:**

1. Follow the same steps as the classic coffee gelato recipe.
2. Once the gelato is churned and creamy, add the chopped pecans and mix until well incorporated. Freeze for at least 2 hours before serving.

**Nutritional values:** Approx 240 kcal per serving (based on 6 servings), 7g protein, 31g carbohydrates, 12g fat

## 134. Coffee and White Chocolate Chip Gelato

**Ingredients:**

- 500 ml of whole milk
- 200 grams of sugar
- 2 tablespoons of instant coffee
- 4 egg yolks
- 100 grams of white chocolate chips

**Directions:**

1. Follow the same steps as the classic coffee gelato recipe.
2. Once the gelato is churned and creamy, add the white chocolate chips and mix until well incorporated. Freeze for at least 2 hours before serving.

**Nutritional values:** Approx 250 kcal per serving (based on 6 servings), 7g protein, 32g carbohydrates, 12g fat

## 135. Espresso and Pistachio Swirl Gelato

Ingredients:

- 500 ml of almond milk
- 200 grams of honey
- 1/4 cup of espresso coffee (or strongly brewed coffee)
- 4 egg yolks
- 100 grams of pistachios, crushed into small chunks

Directions:

1. Heat almond milk in a saucepan until it's steaming but not boiling.
2. In a separate bowl, whisk together the egg yolks and honey until well combined.
3. Slowly pour the hot almond milk into the egg yolk mixture, whisking constantly to prevent the eggs from cooking.
4. Once combined, return the mixture to the saucepan and cook over medium heat, stirring constantly until it thickens into a custard.
5. Remove from heat and stir in the espresso coffee. Allow the mixture to cool.
6. Once cool, pour the mixture into an ice cream maker and churn according to the manufacturer's instructions.
7. When the gelato is almost fully churned, add in the crushed pistachios and let it mix for another few minutes.
8. Transfer the gelato to a lidded container and freeze for at least 2 hours before serving.

Nutritional values: Approx 215 kcal per serving (based on 6 servings), 6g protein, 30g carbohydrates, 10g fat

# 136. Cappuccino and Spiced Rum Gelato

Ingredients:

- 500 ml of half-and-half cream
- 200 grams of brown sugar
- 2 shots of freshly brewed espresso
- 4 egg yolks
- 3 tablespoons of spiced rum

Directions:

1. Warm the half-and-half cream in a saucepan over medium heat until it's just beginning to steam.
2. In a separate bowl, whisk together the egg yolks and brown sugar until they're well combined and the sugar has begun to dissolve.
3. Slowly pour the hot cream into the egg yolk mixture, whisking constantly so the eggs don't cook.
4. Transfer the mixture back to the saucepan and cook over low heat, stirring constantly until the mixture thickens into a custard.
5. Remove the custard from the heat and stir in the freshly brewed espresso. Allow the custard to cool completely.
6. Once cool, stir in the spiced rum.
7. Churn the custard in an ice cream maker according to the manufacturer's instructions.
8. Transfer the gelato to a lidded container and freeze for at least 2 hours before serving.

Nutritional values: Approx 230 kcal per serving (based on 6 servings), 5g protein, 29g carbohydrates, 9g fat

# 137. Mocha and Almond Butter Gelato

Ingredients:

- 500 ml of half-and-half cream
- 200 grams of brown sugar
- 2 tablespoons of instant coffee
- 4 egg yolks
- 2 tablespoons of cocoa powder
- 3 tablespoons of smooth almond butter

Directions:

1. In a medium saucepan, warm the half-and-half cream over medium heat until it begins to steam.
2. In a separate bowl, whisk together the egg yolks, brown sugar, instant coffee, and cocoa powder until well combined and the sugar has begun to dissolve.
3. Gradually add the hot cream to the egg yolk mixture, whisking constantly to prevent the eggs from cooking.
4. Transfer the mixture back to the saucepan and cook over low heat, stirring constantly, until the mixture thickens into a custard.
5. Remove the custard from heat and let it cool completely.
6. Once cool, stir in the almond butter until well incorporated.
7. Churn the mixture in an ice cream maker according to the manufacturer's instructions.
8. Transfer the gelato to a lidded container and freeze for at least 2 hours before serving.

Nutritional values: Approx 240 kcal per serving (based on 6 servings), 6g protein, 29g carbohydrates, 12g fat

# 138. Coffee and Coconut Flakes Gelato

**Ingredients:**

- 500 ml of whole milk
- 200 grams of sugar
- 2 tablespoons of instant coffee
- 4 egg yolks
- 50 grams of coconut flakes

**Directions:**

1. Follow the same steps as the classic coffee gelato recipe.

2. Once the gelato is churned and creamy, add the coconut flakes and mix until well incorporated. Freeze for at least 2 hours before serving.

**Nutritional values:** Approx 210 kcal per serving (based on 6 servings), 6g protein, 31g carbohydrates, 9g fat

# 139. Coffee and Vanilla Bean Gelato

**Ingredients:**

- 500 ml of whole milk
- 200 grams of sugar
- 2 tablespoons of instant coffee
- 4 egg yolks
- 1 vanilla bean, seeds scraped

**Directions:**

1. Follow the same steps as the classic coffee gelato recipe, but add the vanilla bean seeds along with the instant coffee.

**Nutritional values:** Approx 205 kcal per serving (based on 6 servings), 6g protein, 31g carbohydrates, 7g fat

# 140. Coffee and Hazelnut Liqueur Gelato

**Ingredients:**

- 500 ml of whole milk
- 200 grams of sugar
- 2 tablespoons of instant coffee

- 4 egg yolks
- 2 tablespoons of hazelnut liqueur

**Directions:**

1. Follow the same steps as the classic coffee gelato recipe.
2. Once the gelato is churned and creamy, add the hazelnut liqueur and mix until well incorporated. Freeze for at least 2 hours before serving.

**Nutritional values:** Approx 210 kcal per serving (based on 6 servings), 6g protein, 31g carbohydrates, 7g fat

# 141. Coffee and Dulce de Leche Gelato

**Ingredients:**

- 500 ml of whole milk
- 200 grams of sugar
- 2 tablespoons of instant coffee
- 4 egg yolks
- 100 grams of dulce de leche

**Directions:**

1. Follow the same steps as the classic coffee gelato recipe.
2. Once the gelato is churned and creamy, add the dulce de leche and mix until well incorporated. Freeze for at least 2 hours before serving.

**Nutritional values:** Approx 230 kcal per serving (based on 6 servings), 7g protein, 36g carbohydrates, 7g fat

# 142. Turkish Coffee Ice Cream

Ingredients:

- 1 cup whole milk
- 3/4 cup sugar
- 2 cups heavy cream
- 2 tablespoons finely ground Turkish coffee
- 1/2 teaspoon cardamom

Directions:

1. In a medium saucepan, mix together milk and sugar until the sugar is dissolved.
2. Stir in the heavy cream, Turkish coffee, and cardamom.
3. Cook the mixture over medium heat until it begins to steam.
4. Remove from heat and let it cool.
5. Once cooled, pour the mixture into an ice cream maker and churn according to the manufacturer's instructions.
6. Transfer the ice cream to a lidded container and freeze for at least 4 hours before serving.

**Nutritional values:** Approx 220 kcal per serving (based on 6 servings), 2g protein, 15g carbohydrates, 16g fat

# 143. Coffee and Bailey's Gelato

**Ingredients:**

- 500 ml of whole milk
- 200 grams of sugar
- 2 tablespoons of instant coffee

- 4 egg yolks
- 2 tablespoons of Bailey's Irish Cream

**Directions:**

1. Follow the same steps as the classic coffee gelato recipe.
2. Once the gelato is churned and creamy, add the Bailey's and mix until well incorporated. Freeze for at least 2 hours before serving.

**Nutritional values:** Approx 220 kcal per serving (based on 6 servings), 6g protein, 32g carbohydrates, 7g fat

# 144. Coffee and Toasted Marshmallow Gelato

**Ingredients:**

- 500 ml of whole milk
- 200 grams of sugar
- 2 tablespoons of instant coffee
- 4 egg yolks
- 50 grams of mini marshmallows, toasted

**Directions:**

1. Follow the same steps as the classic coffee gelato recipe.
2. Once the gelato is churned and creamy, add the toasted mini marshmallows and mix until well incorporated. Freeze for at least 2 hours before serving.

**Nutritional values:** Approx 210 kcal per serving (based on 6 servings), 6g protein, 33g carbohydrates, 7g fat

# 145. Coffee and Toffee Bits Gelato

**Ingredients:**

- 500 ml of whole milk
- 200 grams of sugar
- 2 tablespoons of instant coffee
- 4 egg yolks
- 50 grams of toffee bits

**Directions:**

1. Follow the same steps as the classic coffee gelato recipe.
2. Once the gelato is churned and creamy, add the toffee bits and mix until well incorporated. Freeze for at least 2 hours before serving.

**Nutritional values:** Approx 220 kcal per serving (based on 6 servings), 6g protein, 34g carbohydrates, 7g fat

# 146. Coffee and Salted Caramel Gelato

**Ingredients:**

- 500 ml of whole milk
- 200 grams of sugar
- 2 tablespoons of instant coffee
- 4 egg yolks
- 100 grams of salted caramel, melted

**Directions:**

1. Follow the same steps as the classic coffee gelato recipe.

2. Once the gelato is churned and creamy, add the melted salted caramel and mix until well incorporated. Freeze for at least 2 hours before serving.

**Nutritional values:** Approx 240 kcal per serving (based on 6 servings), 7g protein, 36g carbohydrates, 9g fat

# 147. Vietnamese Coffee Ice Cream

Ingredients:

- 1 cup sweetened condensed milk
- 1 cup brewed dark roast coffee
- 2 cups heavy cream
- 1/2 cup sugar

Directions:

1. Combine sweetened condensed milk and coffee in a bowl, stirring until well combined.
2. In a separate bowl, whisk heavy cream and sugar until sugar is dissolved.
3. Combine the cream mixture with the coffee mixture and stir until well mixed.
4. Chill the mixture in the refrigerator until cool.
5. Once chilled, pour into an ice cream maker and churn according to the manufacturer's instructions.
6. Transfer to a lidded container and freeze for at least 4 hours before serving.

**Nutritional values:** Approx 230 kcal per serving (based on 6 servings), 3g protein, 20g carbohydrates, 16g fat

# 148. Coffee Toffee Ice Cream

Ingredients:

- 1 cup whole milk
- 3/4 cup sugar
- 2 cups heavy cream
- 2 tablespoons instant coffee granules
- 1/2 cup toffee bits

Directions:

1. In a medium saucepan, mix together milk and sugar until the sugar is dissolved.
2. Stir in the heavy cream and instant coffee.
3. Cook the mixture over medium heat until it begins to steam.
4. Remove from heat, let it cool and stir in the toffee bits.
5. Once cooled, pour the mixture into an ice cream maker and churn according to the manufacturer's instructions.
6. Transfer the ice cream to a lidded container and freeze for at least 4 hours before serving.

**Nutritional values:** Approx 240 kcal per serving (based on 6 servings), 3g protein, 20g carbohydrates, 16g fat

# 149. Coffee and Caramelised Hazelnuts Gelato

**Ingredients:**

- 500 ml of whole milk

- 200 grams of sugar
- 2 tablespoons of instant coffee
- 4 egg yolks
- 100 grams of caramelised hazelnuts, chopped

**Directions:**

1. Follow the same steps as the classic coffee gelato recipe.
2. Once the gelato is churned and creamy, add the caramelised hazelnuts and mix until well incorporated. Freeze for at least 2 hours before serving.

**Nutritional values:** Approx 250 kcal per serving (based on 6 servings), 7g protein, 33g carbohydrates, 12g fat

# 150. Espresso Gelato

Ingredients:

- 1 cup whole milk
- 1/2 cup sugar
- 2 cups heavy cream
- 2 shots of espresso

Directions:

1. In a medium saucepan, mix together milk and sugar until the sugar is dissolved.
2. Stir in the heavy cream and espresso.
3. Cook the mixture over medium heat until it begins to steam.
4. Remove from heat and let it cool.
5. Once cooled, pour the mixture into an ice cream maker and churn according to the manufacturer's instructions.
6. Transfer the gelato to a lidded container and freeze for at least 4 hours before serving.

**Nutritional values:** Approx 220 kcal per serving (based on 6 servings), 2g protein, 14g carbohydrates, 16g fat

# Vegetable Ice Cream

## 151. Spinach and Kiwi Gelato

**Ingredients:**

- 300 ml of whole milk
- 200 grams of sugar
- 2 cups of spinach leaves, washed
- 4 ripe kiwis, peeled and diced

**Directions:**

1. In a blender, combine the spinach leaves, kiwi, milk, and sugar. Blend until smooth.
2. Pour the mixture into an ice cream maker and churn according to the manufacturer's instructions.
3. Once the gelato is creamy and thick, transfer it to a lidded container and freeze for at least 2 hours before serving.

**Nutritional values:** Approx 140 kcal per serving (based on 6 servings), 2g protein, 32g carbohydrates, 2g fat

## 152. Avocado Gelato

**Ingredients:**

- 2 ripe avocados
- 400 ml of whole milk
- 150 grams of sugar

- Juice of one lime

**Directions:**

1. In a blender, combine the avocados, milk, sugar, and lime juice. Blend until smooth.
2. Pour the mixture into an ice cream maker and churn according to the manufacturer's instructions.
3. Once the gelato is creamy and thick, transfer it to a lidded container and freeze for at least 2 hours before serving.

**Nutritional values:** Approx 200 kcal per serving (based on 6 servings), 3g protein, 25g carbohydrates, 12g fat

# 153. Sweet Corn and Honey Gelato

**Ingredients:**

- 3 ears of corn
- 500 ml of whole milk
- 100 grams of sugar
- 2 tablespoons of honey

**Directions:**

1. Remove the kernels from the corn cobs and combine them with the milk in a saucepan.
2. Bring to a simmer over medium heat, then remove from heat and let steep for 1 hour.
3. Strain the mixture through a fine-mesh sieve, pressing down on the kernels to extract as much liquid as possible.
4. Combine the corn-infused milk with the sugar and honey in a blender, and blend until smooth.
5. Pour the mixture into an ice cream maker and churn according to the manufacturer's instructions.

6. Once the gelato is creamy and thick, transfer it to a lidded container and freeze for at least 2 hours before serving.

**Nutritional values:** Approx 180 kcal per serving (based on 6 servings), 4g protein, 34g carbohydrates, 5g fat

# 154. Sweet Potato and Cinnamon Gelato

**Ingredients:**

- 2 large sweet potatoes
- 500 ml of whole milk
- 200 grams of sugar
- 1 teaspoon of cinnamon

**Directions:**

1. Peel and dice the sweet potatoes, then boil them in a pot of water until soft.
2. Drain the sweet potatoes and let them cool slightly, then combine them with the milk, sugar, and cinnamon in a blender.
3. Blend until smooth, then pour the mixture into an ice cream maker and churn according to the manufacturer's instructions.
4. Once the gelato is creamy and thick, transfer it to a lidded container and freeze for at least 2 hours before serving.

**Nutritional values:** Approx 210 kcal per serving (based on 6 servings), 4g protein, 42g carbohydrates, 3g fat

# 155. Zucchini and Mint Gelato

**Ingredients:**

- 2 medium zucchinis
- 400 ml of whole milk
- 150 grams of sugar
- A handful of fresh mint leaves

**Directions:**

1. Cut the zucchinis into chunks and steam them until they're soft.
2. Let the zucchinis cool slightly, then combine them with the milk, sugar, and mint leaves in a blender.
3. Blend until smooth, then pour the mixture into an ice cream maker and churn according to the manufacturer's instructions.
4. Once the gelato is creamy and thick, transfer it to a lidded container and freeze for at least 2 hours before serving.

**Nutritional values:** Approx 130 kcal per serving (based on 6 servings), 3g protein, 28g carbohydrates, 2g fat

# 156. Beetroot and Orange Gelato

**Ingredients:**

- 2 medium beetroots
- Juice of 2 oranges
- 400 ml of whole milk
- 150 grams of sugar

**Directions:**

1. Boil the beetroots until they are tender, then peel and dice them.
2. Combine the beetroot chunks, orange juice, milk, and sugar in a blender.
3. Blend until smooth, then pour the mixture into an ice cream maker and churn according to the manufacturer's instructions.
4. Once the gelato is creamy and thick, transfer it to a lidded container and freeze for at least 2 hours before serving.

**Nutritional values:** Approx 160 kcal per serving (based on 6 servings), 3g protein, 35g carbohydrates, 2g fat

# 157. Pumpkin and Spice Gelato

**Ingredients:**

- 2 cups of pumpkin puree
- 500 ml of whole milk
- 200 grams of sugar
- 1 teaspoon of pumpkin pie spice

**Directions:**

1. Combine the pumpkin puree, milk, sugar, and spice in a blender.
2. Blend until smooth, then pour the mixture into an ice cream maker and churn according to the manufacturer's instructions.
3. Once the gelato is creamy and thick, transfer it to a lidded container and freeze for at least 2 hours before serving.

**Nutritional values:** Approx 210 kcal per serving (based on 6 servings), 4g protein, 42g carbohydrates, 3g fat

## 158. Carrot and Ginger Gelato

**Ingredients:**

- 4 medium carrots
- 1 tablespoon of fresh ginger, grated
- 500 ml of whole milk
- 200 grams of sugar

**Directions:**

1. Steam the carrots until they are soft, then let them cool slightly.
2. Combine the cooked carrots, ginger, milk, and sugar in a blender.
3. Blend until smooth, then pour the mixture into an ice cream maker and churn according to the manufacturer's instructions.
4. Once the gelato is creamy and thick, transfer it to a lidded container and freeze for at least 2 hours before serving.

**Nutritional values:** Approx 200 kcal per serving (based on 6 servings), 4g protein, 38g carbohydrates, 3g fat

## 159. Red Bell Pepper and Basil Gelato

**Ingredients:**

- 2 red bell peppers, seeds removed
- A handful of fresh basil leaves
- 400 ml of whole milk
- 150 grams of sugar

**Directions:**

1. Grill the bell peppers until the skin is charred, then let them cool and peel off the skin.
2. Combine the grilled peppers, basil leaves, milk, and sugar in a blender.
3. Blend until smooth, then pour the mixture into an ice cream maker and churn according to the manufacturer's instructions.
4. Once the gelato is creamy and thick, transfer it to a lidded container and freeze for at least 2 hours before serving.

**Nutritional values:** Approx 140 kcal per serving (based on 6 servings), 3g protein, 30g carbohydrates, 2g fat

## 160. Cucumber and Lime Gelato

**Ingredients:**

- 2 large cucumbers, peeled and seeded
- Juice of 2 limes
- 400 ml of whole milk
- 150 grams of sugar

**Directions:**

1. Combine the cucumbers, lime juice, milk, and sugar in a blender.
2. Blend until smooth, then pour the mixture into an ice cream maker and churn according to the manufacturer's instructions.
3. Once the gelato is creamy and thick, transfer it to a lidded container and freeze for at least 2 hours before serving.

**Nutritional values:** Approx 130 kcal per serving (based on 6 servings), 3g protein, 28g carbohydrates, 2g fat

## 161. Tomato and Basil Gelato

**Ingredients:**

- 4 ripe tomatoes, seeds removed
- A handful of fresh basil leaves
- 400 ml of whole milk
- 150 grams of sugar

**Directions:**

1. Blend the tomatoes, basil leaves, milk, and sugar in a blender until smooth.
2. Pour the mixture into an ice cream maker and churn according to the manufacturer's instructions.
3. Once the gelato is creamy and thick, transfer it to a lidded container and freeze for at least 2 hours before serving.

**Nutritional values:** Approx 140 kcal per serving (based on 6 servings), 3g protein, 30g carbohydrates, 2g fat

## 162. Celery and Apple Gelato

**Ingredients:**

- 4 celery stalks
- 2 apples, cored and chopped
- 400 ml of whole milk
- 150 grams of sugar

**Directions:**

1. Combine the celery, apples, milk, and sugar in a blender.

2. Blend until smooth, then pour the mixture into an ice cream maker and churn according to the manufacturer's instructions.
3. Once the gelato is creamy and thick, transfer it to a lidded container and freeze for at least 2 hours before serving.

**Nutritional values:** Approx 150 kcal per serving (based on 6 servings), 3g protein, 32g carbohydrates, 2g fat

## 163. Kale and Banana Gelato

**Ingredients:**

- 2 cups of kale, washed and stems removed
- 2 ripe bananas
- 400 ml of whole milk
- 150 grams of sugar

**Directions:**

1. Blend the kale, bananas, milk, and sugar in a blender until smooth.
2. Pour the mixture into an ice cream maker and churn according to the manufacturer's instructions.
3. Once the gelato is creamy and thick, transfer it to a lidded container and freeze for at least 2 hours before serving.

**Nutritional values:** Approx 180 kcal per serving (based on 6 servings), 4g protein, 38g carbohydrates, 3g fat

## 164. Pea and Mint Gelato

**Ingredients:**

- 2 cups of peas, fresh or frozen

- A handful of fresh mint leaves
- 400 ml of whole milk
- 150 grams of sugar

**Directions:**

1. If using fresh peas, shell them. If using frozen peas, thaw them.
2. Blend the peas, mint leaves, milk, and sugar in a blender until smooth.
3. Pour the mixture into an ice cream maker and churn according to the manufacturer's instructions.
4. Once the gelato is creamy and thick, transfer it to a lidded container and freeze for at least 2 hours before serving.

**Nutritional values:** Approx 160 kcal per serving (based on 6 servings), 5g protein, 30g carbohydrates, 3g fat

## 165. Fennel and Pear Gelato

**Ingredients:**

- 2 fennel bulbs
- 2 ripe pears, cored and chopped
- 400 ml of whole milk
- 150 grams of sugar

**Directions:**

1. Trim the fennel bulbs and chop them into chunks.
2. Blend the fennel, pears, milk, and sugar in a blender until smooth.
3. Pour the mixture into an ice cream maker and churn according to the manufacturer's instructions.
4. Once the gelato is creamy and thick, transfer it to a lidded container and freeze for at least 2 hours before serving.

**Nutritional values:** Approx 150 kcal per serving (based on 6 servings), 3g protein, 32g carbohydrates, 2g fat

# 166. Zucchini and Lemon Gelato

**Ingredients:**

- 2 medium zucchinis
- Juice of 1 lemon
- 400 ml of whole milk
- 150 grams of sugar

**Directions:**

1. Chop the zucchinis into chunks.
2. Blend the zucchinis, lemon juice, milk, and sugar in a blender until smooth.
3. Pour the mixture into an ice cream maker and churn according to the manufacturer's instructions.
4. Once the gelato is creamy and thick, transfer it to a lidded container and freeze for at least 2 hours before serving.

**Nutritional values:** Approx 140 kcal per serving (based on 6 servings), 3g protein, 30g carbohydrates, 2g fat

# 167. Spinach and Pineapple Gelato

**Ingredients:**

- 2 cups of spinach, washed and stems removed
- 1 cup of pineapple chunks
- 400 ml of whole milk
- 150 grams of sugar

**Directions:**

1. Blend the spinach, pineapple, milk, and sugar in a blender until smooth.
2. Pour the mixture into an ice cream maker and churn according to the manufacturer's instructions.
3. Once the gelato is creamy and thick, transfer it to a lidded container and freeze for at least 2 hours before serving.

**Nutritional values:** Approx 170 kcal per serving (based on 6 servings), 4g protein, 36g carbohydrates, 3g fat

# 168. Butternut Squash and Nutmeg Gelato

**Ingredients:**

- 1 butternut squash, peeled and cubed
- 1 teaspoon of nutmeg
- 500 ml of whole milk
- 200 grams of sugar

**Directions:**

1. Steam or roast the butternut squash until it is soft.
2. Blend the squash, nutmeg, milk, and sugar in a blender until smooth.
3. Pour the mixture into an ice cream maker and churn according to the manufacturer's instructions.
4. Once the gelato is creamy and thick, transfer it to a lidded container and freeze for at least 2 hours before serving.

**Nutritional values:** Approx 220 kcal per serving (based on 6 servings), 4g protein, 45g carbohydrates, 4g fat

# 169. Sweet Corn Ice Cream

Ingredients:

- 2 cups heavy cream
- 1 cup whole milk
- 3/4 cup granulated sugar
- 1 cup fresh sweet corn kernels

Directions:

1. Combine heavy cream, whole milk, and sugar in a medium saucepan and heat over medium heat until sugar is dissolved.
2. Add the sweet corn kernels and bring the mixture to a simmer.
3. Remove from heat and let it sit for 1 hour to infuse the corn flavor.
4. Blend the mixture until smooth and then strain through a fine-mesh sieve, discarding the solids.
5. Chill the mixture in the refrigerator until cool.
6. Once chilled, pour into an ice cream maker and churn according to the manufacturer's instructions.
7. Transfer to a lidded container and freeze for at least 4 hours before serving.

**Nutritional values:** Approx 210 kcal per serving (based on 6 servings), 2g protein, 16g carbohydrates, 16g fat

# 170. Broccoli and Kiwi Gelato

**Ingredients:**

- 2 cups of broccoli florets

- 2 kiwis, peeled
- 400 ml of whole milk
- 150 grams of sugar

**Directions:**

1. Steam the broccoli florets until they are soft, then let them cool slightly.
2. Blend the broccoli, kiwis, milk, and sugar in a blender until smooth.
3. Pour the mixture into an ice cream maker and churn according to the manufacturer's instructions.
4. Once the gelato is creamy and thick, transfer it to a lidded container and freeze for at least 2 hours before serving.

**Nutritional values:** Approx 160 kcal per serving (based on 6 servings), 4g protein, 33g carbohydrates, 3g fat

# 171. Avocado and Lime Gelato

**Ingredients:**

- 2 ripe avocados
- Juice of 2 limes
- 400 ml of whole milk
- 150 grams of sugar

**Directions:**

1. Cut the avocados in half, remove the pit, and scoop out the flesh.
2. Blend the avocado, lime juice, milk, and sugar in a blender until smooth.
3. Pour the mixture into an ice cream maker and churn according to the manufacturer's instructions.

4. Once the gelato is creamy and thick, transfer it to a lidded container and freeze for at least 2 hours before serving.

**Nutritional values:** Approx 210 kcal per serving (based on 6 servings), 3g protein, 30g carbohydrates, 10g fat

# 172. Cucumber and Mint Gelato

**Ingredients:**

- 2 cucumbers
- A handful of fresh mint leaves
- 400 ml of whole milk
- 150 grams of sugar

**Directions:**

1. Peel the cucumbers and chop them into chunks.
2. Blend the cucumbers, mint leaves, milk, and sugar in a blender until smooth.
3. Pour the mixture into an ice cream maker and churn according to the manufacturer's instructions.
4. Once the gelato is creamy and thick, transfer it to a lidded container and freeze for at least 2 hours before serving.

**Nutritional values:** Approx 140 kcal per serving (based on 6 servings), 3g protein, 29g carbohydrates, 2g fat

# 173. Pumpkin and Ginger Gelato

**Ingredients:**

- 1 small pumpkin, peeled and cubed
- 1 teaspoon of ginger, grated

- 500 ml of whole milk
- 200 grams of sugar

**Directions:**

1. Steam or roast the pumpkin until it is soft.
2. Blend the pumpkin, ginger, milk, and sugar in a blender until smooth.
3. Pour the mixture into an ice cream maker and churn according to the manufacturer's instructions.
4. Once the gelato is creamy and thick, transfer it to a lidded container and freeze for at least 2 hours before serving.

**Nutritional values:** Approx 220 kcal per serving (based on 6 servings), 4g protein, 45g carbohydrates, 4g fat

# 174. Spinach and Mint Ice Cream

Ingredients:

- 2 cups spinach leaves
- 1 cup fresh mint leaves
- 1 cup whole milk
- 1 cup heavy cream
- 3/4 cup granulated sugar

Directions:

1. Combine spinach and mint leaves in a blender and puree until smooth.
2. In a medium saucepan, combine whole milk, heavy cream, and sugar, heat over medium heat until sugar is dissolved.
3. Pour the spinach and mint puree into the saucepan and stir until well combined.
4. Chill the mixture in the refrigerator until cool.

5. Once chilled, pour into an ice cream maker and churn according to the manufacturer's instructions.
6. Transfer to a lidded container and freeze for at least 4 hours before serving.

**Nutritional values:** Approx 160 kcal per serving (based on 6 servings), 2g protein, 14g carbohydrates, 11g fat

# 175. Beetroot Raspberry Sorbet

Ingredients:

- 2 large beetroots
- 2 cups fresh raspberries
- 1 cup granulated sugar
- 2 cups water

Directions:

1. Peel and dice the beetroots, then place in a saucepan with water and sugar. Simmer over medium heat until the beetroot is tender.
2. Add the fresh raspberries to the beetroot mixture and stir until well combined.
3. Blend the mixture in a food processor or blender until smooth. Strain through a fine-mesh sieve, discarding the solids.
4. Chill the mixture in the refrigerator until cool.
5. Once chilled, pour into an ice cream maker and churn according to the manufacturer's instructions.
6. Transfer to a lidded container and freeze for at least 4 hours before serving.

**Nutritional values:** Approx 85 kcal per serving (based on 6 servings), 1g protein, 21g carbohydrates, 0.2g fat

# Toppings for Ice Cream

## 176. Chocolate Fudge Sauce

**Ingredients:**

- 1 cup of granulated sugar
- 3/4 cup of unsweetened cocoa powder
- 1/2 cup of milk
- 1/4 cup of butter
- 1 teaspoon of vanilla extract

**Directions:**

1. In a medium saucepan, combine sugar and cocoa powder.
2. Stir in milk and butter and cook over medium heat until the butter is melted and the mixture is smooth.
3. Remove from heat and stir in vanilla extract.
4. Allow to cool slightly before drizzling over ice cream.

**Calories:** Approx 100 kcal per serving (2 tablespoons)

## 177. Salted Caramel Sauce

**Ingredients:**

- 1 cup of granulated sugar
- 1/4 cup of water
- 3/4 cup of heavy cream
- 3 tablespoons of unsalted butter

- 1 teaspoon of sea salt

**Directions:**

1. In a medium saucepan, combine sugar and water.
2. Heat over medium-high heat, stirring until sugar is dissolved.
3. Stop stirring and allow the mixture to boil until it becomes a deep amber color.
4. Remove from heat and slowly whisk in cream, followed by butter and salt.
5. Allow to cool before drizzling over ice cream.

**Calories:** Approx 130 kcal per serving (2 tablespoons)

# 178. Berry Compote

**Ingredients:**

- 2 cups of mixed berries (fresh or frozen)
- 1/4 cup of granulated sugar
- Juice of 1 lemon

**Directions:**

1. In a medium saucepan, combine berries, sugar, and lemon juice.
2. Cook over medium heat until the berries burst and release their juices, and the mixture thickens, about 10-15 minutes.
3. Allow to cool before spooning over ice cream.

**Calories:** Approx 50 kcal per serving (2 tablespoons)

## 179. Toasted Coconut Flakes

**Ingredients:**

- 1 cup of unsweetened coconut flakes

**Directions:**

1. Preheat oven to 325°F (163°C).
2. Spread coconut flakes on a baking sheet in a thin layer.
3. Bake for 5-10 minutes, stirring occasionally, until golden brown.
4. Allow to cool before sprinkling over ice cream.

**Calories:** Approx 70 kcal per serving (2 tablespoons)

## 180. Praline Pecans

**Ingredients:**

- 1 cup of pecan halves
- 1/4 cup of brown sugar
- 1 tablespoon of butter
- Pinch of salt

**Directions:**

1. Preheat oven to 350°F (177°C) and line a baking sheet with parchment paper.
2. In a medium bowl, melt the butter and stir in the brown sugar and salt.

3. Add the pecans and toss to coat.
4. Spread pecans in a single layer on the prepared baking sheet.
5. Bake for 10-15 minutes, stirring occasionally, until toasted and aromatic.
6. Allow to cool before crumbling over ice cream.

**Calories:** Approx 90 kcal per serving (2 tablespoons)

# 181. Peanut Butter Drizzle

**Ingredients:**

- 1/2 cup of smooth peanut butter
- 3 tablespoons of honey
- 2-4 tablespoons of milk

**Directions:**

1. In a small saucepan, combine peanut butter and honey over medium heat.
2. Stir until well combined and heated through.
3. Gradually add milk, one tablespoon at a time, until you reach your desired consistency.
4. Allow to cool slightly before drizzling over ice cream.

**Calories:** Approx 110 kcal per serving (2 tablespoons)

# 182. Rainbow Sprinkles

**Ingredients:**

- Ready-made rainbow sprinkles

**Directions:**

1. Simply sprinkle over your ice cream for a pop of color and a sweet, crunchy texture. No preparation needed.

**Calories:** Approx 20 kcal per serving (1 tablespoon)

## 183. Cherry Sauce

**Ingredients:**

- 2 cups of cherries, pitted and halved
- 1/2 cup of granulated sugar
- Juice of half a lemon

**Directions:**

1. In a medium saucepan, combine cherries, sugar, and lemon juice.
2. Cook over medium heat until the cherries burst and release their juices, and the mixture thickens, about 10-15 minutes.
3. Allow to cool before spooning over ice cream.

**Calories:** Approx 60 kcal per serving (2 tablespoons)

## 184. Candied Almonds

**Ingredients:**

- 1 cup of almonds, chopped
- 1/4 cup of granulated sugar
- 1 tablespoon of butter

**Directions:**

1. In a medium skillet, melt the butter over medium heat.

2. Add the sugar and almonds, stirring to coat the almonds in the melted sugar-butter mixture.
3. Continue to cook, stirring often, until the sugar has caramelized and the almonds are toasted.
4. Allow to cool before sprinkling over ice cream.

**Calories:** Approx 90 kcal per serving (2 tablespoons)

# 185. Whipped Cream

**Ingredients:**

- 1 cup of heavy cream
- 2 tablespoons of powdered sugar
- 1 teaspoon of vanilla extract

**Directions:**

1. In a large bowl, whip the cream until soft peaks form.
2. Add the powdered sugar and vanilla, and continue to whip until stiff peaks form.
3. Spoon or pipe onto ice cream as desired.

**Calories:** Approx 60 kcal per serving (2 tablespoons)

# 186. Marshmallow Fluff

**Ingredients:**

- 1 jar of ready-made marshmallow fluff

**Directions:**

1. Simply spoon or pipe the marshmallow fluff onto your ice cream. It's especially delicious when lightly toasted with a kitchen torch.

**Calories:** Approx 40 kcal per serving (1 tablespoon)

# 187. Mocha Drizzle

**Ingredients:**

- 1/2 cup of strong brewed coffee
- 1/4 cup of granulated sugar
- 2 tablespoons of unsweetened cocoa powder

**Directions:**

1. In a small saucepan, combine the coffee, sugar, and cocoa powder.
2. Stir over medium heat until the sugar has dissolved and the sauce is heated through.
3. Allow to cool slightly before drizzling over ice cream.

**Calories:** Approx 30 kcal per serving (1 tablespoon)

# 188. Oreo Cookie Crumble

**Ingredients:**

- 12 Oreo cookies

**Directions:**

1. Place the cookies in a zip-top bag and crush them into fine crumbs using a rolling pin or the bottom of a sturdy glass.

2. Sprinkle the crumbs over your ice cream.

**Calories:** Approx 50 kcal per serving (1 tablespoon)

# 189. White Chocolate Chips

**Ingredients:**

- Ready-made white chocolate chips

**Directions:**

1. Simply sprinkle the chips over your ice cream. If you want them to be melty, heat them in the microwave for a few seconds first.

**Calories:** Approx 70 kcal per serving (1 tablespoon)

# 190. Cinnamon-Sugar Pecans

**Ingredients:**

- 1 cup of pecans
- 1/4 cup of granulated sugar
- 1 tablespoon of unsalted butter, melted
- 1/2 teaspoon of ground cinnamon

**Directions:**

1. Preheat your oven to 350°F (175°C) and line a baking sheet with parchment paper.
2. In a bowl, toss the pecans with the melted butter.
3. In another bowl, combine the sugar and cinnamon.
4. Add the sugar mixture to the pecans and toss until they're coated.

5. Spread the pecans on your prepared baking sheet in a single layer.
6. Bake for 10-15 minutes, stirring occasionally, until the pecans are toasted and aromatic.
7. Let them cool before crumbling over your ice cream.

**Calories:** Approx 80 kcal per serving (1 tablespoon)

## 191. Brownie Bites

**Ingredients:**

- 2 cups of brownie bites, store-bought or homemade

**Directions:**

1. Cut the brownies into small, bite-sized pieces.
2. Scatter over your ice cream.

**Calories:** Approx 90 kcal per serving (2 tablespoons)

## 192. Mint Syrup

**Ingredients:**

- 1 cup of sugar
- 1 cup of water
- 1/2 cup of fresh mint leaves

**Directions:**

1. In a saucepan, combine sugar, water, and mint leaves.
2. Bring to a boil, then reduce heat and simmer for about 10 minutes.

3. Strain out mint leaves and let the syrup cool.
4. Drizzle over your ice cream.

**Calories:** Approx 60 kcal per serving (1 tablespoon)

# 193. Crushed Peppermint Candy

**Ingredients:**

- 1 cup of peppermint candies

**Directions:**

1. Place the candies in a zip-top bag.
2. Using a rolling pin or the bottom of a sturdy glass, crush the candies into small pieces.
3. Sprinkle the candy pieces over your ice cream.

**Calories:** Approx 70 kcal per serving (1 tablespoon)

# 194. Banana Slices

**Ingredients:**

- 2 bananas

**Directions:**

1. Peel the bananas and slice into rounds.
2. Scatter the banana slices over your ice cream.

**Calories:** Approx 45 kcal per serving (2 tablespoons)

# 195. Crumbled Graham Crackers

**Ingredients:**

- 1 cup of graham crackers

**Directions:**

1. Place the graham crackers in a zip-top bag.
2. Using a rolling pin or the bottom of a sturdy glass, crush the crackers into crumbs.
3. Sprinkle the crumbs over your ice cream.

**Calories:** Approx 60 kcal per serving (1 tablespoon)

# 196. Matcha Sauce

**Ingredients:**

- 1 cup of water
- 1 cup of sugar
- 2 tablespoons of matcha green tea powder

**Directions:**

1. In a saucepan, combine water and sugar.
2. Bring to a simmer and stir until sugar has dissolved.
3. Remove from heat and whisk in matcha powder until smooth.
4. Let cool before drizzling over ice cream.

**Calories:** Approx 60 kcal per serving (1 tablespoon)

# 197. Pistachio Crunch

**Ingredients:**

- 1 cup of pistachios, shells removed
- 2 tablespoons of honey

**Directions:**

1. Toast pistachios in a dry skillet over medium heat until lightly golden and fragrant.
2. Remove from heat and stir in honey until pistachios are well-coated.
3. Allow to cool before sprinkling over ice cream.

**Calories:** Approx 70 kcal per serving (1 tablespoon)

# 198. Coconut Flakes

**Ingredients:**

- 1 cup of unsweetened coconut flakes

**Directions:**

1. Toast coconut flakes in a dry skillet over medium heat until golden and fragrant.
2. Allow to cool before sprinkling over ice cream.

**Calories:** Approx 45 kcal per serving (1 tablespoon)

# 199. Spiced Honey Nut Topping

Ingredients:

- 1 cup mixed nuts (such as almonds, pecans, walnuts, and hazelnuts)
- 2 tablespoons honey
- 1 tablespoon butter
- 1/4 teaspoon ground cinnamon
- 1/8 teaspoon ground nutmeg
- A pinch of salt

Directions:

1. Preheat your oven to 350°F (175°C) and line a baking sheet with parchment paper.
2. In a medium saucepan, melt the butter over medium heat. Stir in the honey, cinnamon, nutmeg, and salt until well combined.
3. Add the mixed nuts to the saucepan and stir until they are evenly coated with the honey mixture.
4. Spread the nut mixture onto the prepared baking sheet in an even layer.
5. Bake in the preheated oven for 10-15 minutes, or until the nuts are toasted and fragrant. Be sure to stir the nuts halfway through the baking time to ensure they toast evenly.
6. Allow the nuts to cool completely. They will become crunchy as they cool.
7. Once cool, break apart any large clusters and use as a topping for ice cream, yogurt, or desserts of your choice.

**Calories:** Approx 115 kcal per serving (1 tablespoon)

# 200. Fresh Berries

**Ingredients:**

- 2 cups of mixed berries (raspberries, strawberries, blueberries, etc.)

**Directions:**

1. Rinse and dry the berries. If using strawberries, remove the hulls and quarter them.
2. Scatter the berries over your ice cream.

**Calories:** Approx 30 kcal per serving (2 tablespoons)

# 201. Caramelized Bananas

**Ingredients:**

- 2 bananas, sliced into rounds
- 2 tablespoons of butter
- 2 tablespoons of brown sugar

**Directions:**

1. In a skillet, melt the butter over medium heat.
2. Add the banana slices and brown sugar, stirring to coat the bananas in the butter and sugar.
3. Cook until the bananas are caramelized and the sugar is bubbling, about 5 minutes.
4. Allow to cool slightly before serving over ice cream.

**Calories:** Approx 100 kcal per serving (2 tablespoons)

# 202. Cookie Dough Bites

**Ingredients:**

- 1 cup of edible cookie dough, store-bought or homemade

**Directions:**

1. Scoop the cookie dough into small, bite-sized pieces.
2. Scatter the cookie dough bites over your ice cream.

**Calories:** Approx 120 kcal per serving (2 tablespoons)

# 203. Blueberry Sauce

**Ingredients:**

- 2 cups of fresh or frozen blueberries
- 1/2 cup of granulated sugar
- 1 tablespoon of lemon juice

**Directions:**

1. In a saucepan, combine the blueberries, sugar, and lemon juice.
2. Bring to a simmer over medium heat and cook until the blueberries burst and the sauce thickens, about 10 minutes.
3. Allow to cool before serving over ice cream.

**Calories:** Approx 70 kcal per serving (2 tablespoons)

## 204. Coconut Whipped Cream

**Ingredients:**

- 1 can of full-fat coconut milk, refrigerated overnight
- 2 tablespoons of powdered sugar
- 1 teaspoon of vanilla extract

**Directions:**

1. Open the can of coconut milk and scoop out the solid cream on top, leaving the liquid behind.
2. In a large bowl, whip the coconut cream until soft peaks form.
3. Add the powdered sugar and vanilla, and continue to whip until stiff peaks form.
4. Spoon or pipe onto ice cream as desired.

**Calories:** Approx 50 kcal per serving (2 tablespoons)

## 205. Pomegranate Seeds

**Ingredients:**

- 1 cup of pomegranate seeds

**Directions:**

1. Simply scatter the pomegranate seeds over your ice cream for a burst of juicy flavor and crunch.

**Calories:** Approx 30 kcal per serving (1 tablespoon)

www.ingramcontent.com/pod-product-compliance
Lightning Source LLC
Chambersburg PA
CBHW071503080526
44587CB00014B/2200